RUTH
ESTHER
JONAH
Johanna W. H. Bos

KNOX PREACHING GUIDES
John H. Hayes, Editor

John Knox Press
ATLANTA

Unless otherwise indicated Scripture quotations are translations from the Hebrew by the author.

Library of Congress Cataloging-in-Publication Data

Bos, Johanna W. H.
  Ruth, Esther, Jonah.

  (Knox preaching guides)
  Bibliography: p.
  1. Bible. O.T. Ruth—Commentaries. 2. Bible.
O.T. Esther—Commentaries. 3. Bible. O.T. Jonah—
Commentaries. 4. Bible. O.T. Ruth—Homiletical use.
5. Bible. O.T. Esther—Homiletical use. 6. Bible.
O.T. Jonah—Homiletical use. I. Title. II. Series.
BS1315.3.B67 1986   222'.3506   85-45793
ISBN 0-8042-3227-X (pbk.)

Contents

Introduction

How do the biblical authors say what they say? This question concerns all who are interested in understanding the Bible and proclaiming it. During the last decade a number of biblical scholars have become engaged in the enterprise of producing literary analysis of the Bible. In this type of scholarship the literature of the Bible is critically analyzed in the same manner as any other body of literature. Their representatives maintain that such a scrutiny, important in the evaluation of all literature, is of crucial importance when we are dealing with religious literature. Robert Alter has argued that "we shall come much closer to the range of intended meanings—theological, psychological, moral, or whatever—of the biblical tale by understanding precisely how it is told" (p. 179).

Much of the material in the Bible was written in the form of narrative; thus the story is a common vehicle in which biblical meaning is expressed. One of the tasks before us is to analyze precisely *how* the stories of Ruth, Esther, and Jonah are shaped, so that we may better understand *what* they have to say.

I Have Heard That Story Before

One of the drawbacks of a tale is that we may already know it, or think we already know it. We have heard it before; it is old hat. The effect of such an attitude is a boredom which sets in among the listeners before the preacher has begun the sermon. That we have heard the story before can certainly be said of the books studied in this volume. If we think in terms of a landscape, both preacher and congregation know the landscape, its contours, its pleasant groves and slippery places. We have been there. The mind's eye conjures up the appropriate pictures: Ruth among the harvesters, Jonah in a storm-tossed sea or in a fish, Esther in a royal palace.

One of the surprises of stories is that they usually hold something unexpected. There are places in the landscape which we had not discovered. As a matter of fact, the better we think we know the story the more unfamiliar it may be in truth. This is especially so with stories that have religious meaning because thay tend to be treated more reverently than other tales and thus, contrary to what was intended, they lose freshness and power. It will help if we can set aside our assumptions about the material before we begin our analysis. Let us assume that there is much here that we have not encountered before.

The distance between us and the stories of the Bible is, after all, immense. We are entering a landscape in which much is unfamiliar to us by virtue of the difference in time and place. A first step then is to become aware of the distance between us and the story once told; the next step is to do everything we can to overcome this distance. We therefore ask all the questions of a text that have to do with the time and the place in which it originated, with the possible process by which it was transmitted and possibly edited, and with the traditions that shaped it and in their turn were shaped by it. Above all, we ask what literary rules, tastes, and conventions dominate the story; for we may have little notion, from our context as listeners and readers, what these literary features were.

Three Stories

Ruth, Esther, and Jonah between them may well span almost the entire period in which the literature contained in the OT took shape. They share the characteristics of being called after their main character, and of presenting a discrete and complete story.

The three show different types of Hebrew narrative: Ruth is probably most aptly called a historical novel, or novella, Esther belongs under the category of folk- or fairy tale, and Jonah under that of parable.

Ruth and Esther both present what is technically called a "comic plot." In such a story the main character is introduced under normal or prosperous conditions, then faces certain obstacles and comes out well in the end. The main part of the story is taken up by the middle which comprises the surmounting of the obstacles. Jonah only partially fits this scheme in that it may have a double plot with the outcome of the second plot left unresolved.

The theological interests of the books are quite different. In Ruth the concerns which shaped the story have to do with the manner in which people should live the life of "covenant devotion." Though there is no report of direct divine intervention, God is clearly experienced as present by the characters. God is seen as the giver of food and life (Ruth 1:6; 4:13). A more secular interest at work in Ruth is the interest in the lineage of King David.

The concern in Esther is with an occasion of the survival of God's people against all odds in harrowing times, and with the continued celebration of that occasion in the feast of Purim. Not only is there no report of divine intervention, there is no mention of God at all. The lack of an obvious theological interest in Esther makes it difficult preaching material. In contrast, the concern in Jonah is with the mercy of God and the survival of the wicked. Unlike Esther it is full of God's word and work. Compared with Esther, both Jonah and Ruth are universalistic in outlook. I believe it to be a mistake to date this concern in post-exilic times, in opposition to the nationalistic policies of, for example, Ezra and Nehemiah. The conviction that the God of Israel is the God of the world and of all peoples is a thread which is woven into the very fabric of Israel's early faith.

Guideposts

We approach these books with certain familiar questions. When were they first told and in which environment? When were they written down, and are the answers to these two questions different? With all three books we can only make an educated guess at an answer; this has the advantage of leaving the imagination free to play with the various possibilities.

What theological traditions are present in the story? How are these developed? What is the larger biblical and historical context of these traditions? These and other questions are the guideposts which we follow in our study of the text.

There are also guideposts to be followed in the literary landscape. First of all there are the *words* of a text. Repetitions, variations, and omissions of certain words are important for the recognition of the particular interests of the story.

Secondly, there is what may be called *narrative technique*. Under this heading we inquire into the manner in which the events are reported. How are certain conventions of story-telling used? How does the action of the story move from component to component?

We will pay special attention to *dialogue*, since this is typically crucial for an understanding of the development of character and events of a Hebrew narrative. Are lines of the dialogue repeated? Are there variations in the repetitions? Are questions only seemingly answered?

Last, we consider the *thematic* development of the story and how it is supported by the considerations already listed here. What are the major themes of the story and how are they developed?

Perspective

Obviously, this factor, though mentioned last, is not the least important. We, as listeners and proclaimers, come to the text within the context of our time, our faith, and our culture. You might say that we approach it with our commitments, prejudices, and expectations. These factors, broadly termed "perspective," should be recognized and owned in order that the engagement with the text may be a productive one. If we deny our perspective existence, insisting on the possibility of objectivity, the chances are that the perspective will exercise unrecognized and ungoverned control over our reading of the text.

Let one example suffice. One of the best known texts from the book of Ruth is in chapter one, vss. 16–17. Here it is recorded that Ruth told Naomi not to go on pleading with her to return to Moab. "For," she states, "where you go, I go, where you lodge, I will lodge; your people, my people . . ." etc. A favorite occasion for the use of these verses is the marriage service, the operative perspective presumably being that words which present the bonding of one person to another are especially appropriate for such an occasion.

There are several objections one could raise against this interpretation as one who has learned that the original context of the biblical material and the meaning which the material once had should be brought to bear on the interpretation of a text. In other words, contemporary training is part of our perspective. The objections, however, become more sharply focused when we become aware of the position from which Ruth was speaking. This position is apparent when we look at the text from the perspective of those who believe that patriarchy is not a part of God's intention for the creation. We all live in a patriarchal culture. If we have begun to grasp the ramifications of this fact for women we can begin to see what Ruth actually dared to say and do. In a world where male support is vital to one's existence, a widow is at the bottom of the heap. Widows are, with orphans, in the Bible always on the lists of those who need special care and justice accorded to them. Ruth allies herself, as such a person without strength, to another such person. She says in so many words, "I'll stay with you at the bottom of the heap." The words of Ruth are witness to one person's alliance to another *in extremis*. These insights make one at least uncomfortable with an easy insertion of Ruth's words into the marriage service. One could argue that in the case of this text the tradition has accorded the text the legitimation it needs in order to be used in the context of a marriage. Yet, it should be clear that this custom arose because in an earlier day the emphasis in interpretation did not lie on the thorough break with tradition as it is presented in Ruth 1:16–17. The concerns of our day, on the other hand, help us to pay attention to Ruth in her social/cultural context and to understand her words from within that context. The more aware we are of our own context the greater the opportunity for a lively engagment with the text. We are today more interested than before in women as they are recorded in the Bible. We are therefore interested in Ruth herself, in her character. We are not satisfied with the blurred image of one who gracefully bends behind the harvesters. Does she give evidence of independence from the restrictions imposed upon her by her culture, and if so, what does this independence teach us about the way in which full partnership between men and women is lived out among God's people?

According to scholars who approach the Bible from a liberation perspective, the problem in regard to our understanding of the biblical text is not our coming to the text with an ideology but rather the amount of unspoken control this ideology exercises over the text. "With ideology is meant a non-pejorative indication of a particular point-of-view toward reality which each person has. It is not a question of whether or not one has an ideology. Everyone does. The question is what is one's ideology" (Joseph L. Hardegree, Jr., *The Bible and Liberation*, p. 99).

RUTH

Introduction

For a book which is often termed "peaceful" or "idyllic," Ruth has attracted some striking controversies among scholars. There is today little agreement on the time and place of its origin, on its importance, or on its literary category. On the other hand Ruth has existed as a kind of forgotten text in the life of the church. Before current changes were made one would have looked in vain for its presence in available lectionaries. Neither did Ruth receive a great deal of attention in standard commentaries and the academic curriculum. Yet, in preaching and teaching from this book one finds it full of riches, and we may consider ourselves fortunate to find Ruth in the current lectionary.

Date

It is not so much the debate surrounding the original date of Ruth which is remarkable as the wide divergence of dates assigned to this text. For a long time it was a fairly common assumption to understand Ruth as a statement of opposition to the removal of foreign wives from the midst of the people under Ezra and Nehemiah. This would place the writing during the fifth century B.C. It was not uncommon to assign an even later date and to suggest for example the third century as a reasonable possibility for its origin. At the same time there were those who simply assumed the book dated from the period of the Judges or shortly thereafter, as the book itself suggests.

The opinion of neither group rested on a close scrutiny of

the book and its place within the literature of the Bible. Recently, a very early date has been advocated. In his commentary, E. F. Campbell proposes the early ninth century with possible earlier origins in the tenth century. For the intricacies of the debate one is advised to consult Campbell. Here it must be sufficient to say that in the opinion of this author a better case can be made for an early rather than a late date, perhaps the first half of the ninth century.

In taking this position much weight is attached to linguistic and literary considerations which show the story to have much in common with the Joseph Cycle (Gen 37, 39—48, 50), with the story about Tamar within that cycle (Gen 38), and with the so-called Court History of David (2 Sam 9—20 and 1 Kings 1—2).

In addition, the book is not easily understood as a polemic tract. The concerns it addresses have to do with the way in which people show one another "kindness," or *hesed*, in their everyday life. This type of concern could be viewed as perennial in the life of Israel, but one can certainly allow for periods in which the concern would become especially acute. When the presence of God is less visible in "signs and wonders" than in an earlier day, people may more readily question the manner in which God is present. In Ruth, as we shall see, God is viewed as present and at work for the good through the faithful actions of people toward each other.

Canonical Place

The position of Ruth in the canon is somewhat fluid, a witness perhaps to the uncertain place of this book in our preaching and teaching. In the translations which follow the ordering of the biblical books found in ancient Greek and Latin versions, Ruth is placed between Judges and 1 Samuel. There we find it in our English translations. In the common Jewish tradition, Ruth is placed in the so-called Writings, the third part of the Hebrew Bible, made up of a collection of various books (e.g., Psalms, Proverbs, Job, etc). In the Jewish tradition Ruth also belongs to the so-called five Scrolls or *Megilloth*, with the Song of Songs, Lamentations, Ecclesiastes, and Esther. Each of these scrolls is read at a particular festival; Ruth, during the Feast of Weeks.

The internal order of these five books varies, but in the standard form of the Hebrew Bible, Ruth follows Proverbs. The content of Prov 31 certainly provides a logical link with Ruth. This chapter of Proverbs sings the praise of a "worthy woman" (Hebrew 'eshet hayl). The book Ruth describes such a woman. Ruth is even called 'eshet hayl (3:11). All of the qualities admired in Prov 31—of determination, hard work, generosity, wisdom, and a sense of humor—are qualities which belong to Ruth.

Theology

What traditions of Israel's faith are at work in this book? The most important idea and the "biggest" is that of redemption. Redemption was a rich concept in Israel, relating to the social as well as the religious intercourse of daily life.

Basically, redemption, in whatever sphere of life, points to the responsibility people have to one another; especially the responsibility of the strong and powerful for the weak and unprotected, those who cannot take responsibility for themselves. Redemption secures the ongoing life of the people as a community, not just as a collection of individuals.

When the concept of redemption is applied to God, the idea of responsibility is equally essential. A basic tenet of Israel's faith is that God is responsible for the people's welfare. God is held accountable when things do not go well with the community or with the individual. Naomi can therefore bitterly complain about God and hold God accountable for her loss of life and hope.

Ruth stresses above all things the crucial importance of a correct understanding of human cooperation with God's grace and favor. Campbell calls this "the correspondence between the way God acts and the way the people in the story act" (p. 29). In a bold way this idea is stated in the first chapter when Naomi wishes for the two Moabite women that the Lord may show them the same "devotion which you have shown to the dead and to me" (1:8). It almost sounds as if God should take a cue from the women on how to behave instead of vice versa; and in view of Naomi's indictment of God this notion is not as farfetched as one might think.

It is at least implied here that two women, and non-Israelites at that, provide an appropriate model for God. In any case throughout the book the emphasis in on how people interact with one another in a way that properly belongs to the life of God's people.

In chapter two, Boaz kindly wishes on Ruth the recompense of God, "the God of Israel," he says, "under whose wings you have come to take refuge" (2:13). In the next episode Ruth neatly turns those words on Boaz when she asks him to "spread your wings over your servant," calling him to his responsibility, "for," she says, "you are a redeemer." In other words, the divine protection is brought into active operation for her by another human being.

So indeed does Ruth function to Naomi. Even though in a literal sense only men could exercise the rights and duties of a redeemer, Ruth acts as a redeemer toward Naomi. She takes responsibility for keeping her company and thus for her loneliness (1:16–17); she makes herself responsible for their livelihood (2:2); and ultimately for the move toward the successful unfolding of the events when she confronts Boaz on the threshing floor (3:9). When the child is born to Ruth and given to Naomi, the neighbors bless the Lord "who has not withheld a redeemer from you today" (4:14).

The book has excellent possibilities for expanding our concept of redemption. Since this idea for us belongs almost exclusively to the theological domain, we do well to scrutinize its roots in the human environment, and for this Ruth provides a good opportunity. We should be careful in this exercise not to get bogged down in forensic details, though some interesting legal customs may well be represented in chapter four. It is not so much the details of the law as the concept which underlies the laws concerning redemption which promises to bear fruit in our explorations. There is a direct line to Jesus Christ here, as elsewhere in the book, since in Christ the notion of God as Israel's Redeemer is brought into active operation for the whole world. Ruth and other characters in this brief story show us something about the "way of redemption." Ruth is a gift of grace to us, latecomers to Israel's faith. She may in a sense be called a type of Christ and, as Tamar (Gen 38) before her, provides a crucial link in the chain that leads to Jesus.

Literary Structure

Following the guideposts outlined in the introduction, we shall briefly survey the importance of key words in the book. In accord with the emphasis on redemption, the root of "redeem" and its derivations sounds one of the main motifs in the narrative. It first occurs at the end of chapter two when Naomi reveals to Ruth that Boaz is "one of our redeemers" (2:20). This fact is anticipated at the beginning of the chapter where Boaz is introduced as a "kinsman" of Elimelech, Naomi's husband. That Boaz is indeed in the line of redeemers is withheld until later, a device typical for Hebrew narrative. To heighten suspense and increase the entertainment, crucial information is held back in the narration and revealed later in the dialogue. Thus, the information that there is someone else who has redemption rights before Boaz does not come out until the conversation between Ruth and Boaz at the grainheap (3:12).

At the pivotal turn of events on the threshing floor the word *redeemer* is used by Ruth when she calls on Boaz as a redeemer (3:9). Boaz, in his reply, uses the word no less than five times (3:11–13). Finally, the word dominates the negotiations at the city gate between Boaz and the near-redeemer. In the first eight verses of chapter four the root for redeem occurs thirteen times. It finds a satisfactory conclusion in vs. 14 in the mouth of the neighbors to whom Naomi had so bitterly complained in chapter one. They point out that God has not "withheld a redeemer" from Naomi. The subject of this phrase as well as the next is likely deliberately vague, in order not to limit the word *redeemer*. God is at least alluded to as redeemer here, but so is the newborn child, as well as Ruth, as well as Boaz.

Unfortunately, the frequency of this word is not reflected in the RSV, which moves from "kinsman" to "relative" to "next of kin" to "redeem" (when the verb is used) with seeming indiscrimination. Of the translations consulted by this author the New International Version and the Jewish Publication Society of America translation most accurately reflect the Hebrew. To get a sense of the way in which this key word is used the Hebrew text must be consulted.

About the narrative technique we can initially observe the

following: the book is easily divided into four episodes or scenes according to its four chapters. In this division the first and the last chapters stand in balance to each other, forming the framework around chapters two and three in which the course of events is worked out decisively. In view of this clear division it would be wise to preach on the entire book, if possible, divided over four sermons.

The balance between chapters one and four is one of contrast. For example, the death of the family members in the first five verses of the book contrasts with the successful union of Ruth and Boaz and the birth of a child in chapter four. In chapter one a cast of characters is stripped from the stage until only two women are left. On entering Bethlehem the community of women is rejected by Naomi. In chapter four there are lively transactions at the city gate, the community of women surround Naomi, the child is in her lap, and there is the joyous occasion of name-giving.

The narrator alternately speeds up and slows down the time in which the events take place. In the first chapter a long period of time goes by in a few verses. When the focus is fully on Naomi, time slows down to a moment on the road when her exchange with Orpah and Ruth takes place. In chapter two time slows down in a significant meeting between Boaz and Ruth, to speed up again at the end of the chapter with the reference to the "end of the barley harvest." In chapter three there is no introduction and conclusion by the narrator. Rather, Naomi's remarks open and close the chapter. The last word of chapter three is "today." Events are speeding up dramatically. We are moved without appropriate transitions from Naomi's last words to the events at the city gate.

In the fourth chapter the focus is on two scenes: the negotiations concerning the redemption of Naomi's property, and Naomi with the child in her lap. In between these two episodes one brief sentence summarizes a period of fair length: "Boaz took Ruth and she became his wife, he entered her, the Lord gave her pregnancy and she gave birth to a son" (4:13). Almost unnoticeably and with subtlety the narrator has used the convention of the "barren wife." Only with the phrase "the Lord gave her pregnancy" does the listener realize that Ruth had not exactly shown great promise as a mother-to-be, having produced no children during the ten years of her marriage to Mahlon.

Dialogue is used in the story, as it is elsewhere in Hebrew narrative, to reveal people's feelings which are only alluded to in the narration. For example, in the first chapter the narrator alludes to Naomi's state of mind by emphasizing her loneliness with the repetition of the word "left behind" (vss. 3 and 5; RSV "left" and "bereft" respectively). Yet her feelings concerning her loneliness are only fully made clear in two subsequent speeches (vss. 11–13 and 20–21). Speech is also used to reveal information, such as the facts concerning the redeemers. Character and relationships are developed through speech. Ruth's determination and courage are only completely made clear with her words to Boaz at the grainheap; her love for Naomi is revealed by the words of the neighbors at the very end of the book (4:15).

Thematically, the overall structure shows a thorough balance. In chapters 1 and 4, contrasting themes are worked out in terms of emptiness/fullness, or death/life. In the first chapter, death intervenes in the life of a family to the point of leaving, in the center of the stage, the weakest members without hope of a future. Naomi points to this lack of promise of life ("have I yet sons in my womb?" 1:11), to her emptiness ("empty the Lord brings me back," 1:21), and to God as the cause of her bitterness ("the hand of the Lord goes forth against me," 1:13).In the last chapter, life and hope for the future stand in contrast to the themes of the first chapter. A son is born to Ruth and Boaz, who is given to Naomi ("a son is born to Naomi!" 4:17); this child is a promise of hope for the future (" a restorer of life and provider in your old age," 4:15), and it is God who is praised on account of the successful outcome of the events ("Blessed be the Lord," 4:14). Over against the silence which meets Ruth's promise of faithfulness ("she refrained from speaking to her," 1:18) stands the praise of Naomi's daughter-in-law in the last chapter ("your daughter-in-law who loves you," 4:15).

In general, there is the contrast of the lonely road from Moab to Judah with the busy comings and goings at the city gate and with the community of women who surround the formerly "left behind" Naomi.

Chapter two corresponds to the third chapter in structure

and *dramatis personae*: a dialogue between Naomi and Ruth surrounds a meeting between Ruth and Boaz. Chapter three has no descriptive introduction or conclusion. The story has become more terse.

Some key contrasts between the two chapters are: in the first dialogue between the two women Naomi responds to Ruth with very few words ("Go, my daughter," 2:21); in the opening dialogue of chapter three Naomi takes the initiative and Ruth is the responder (" All that you say I will do," 3:5). In chapter two everything takes place in the light, in the open field, in public; in the next chapter it is dark, the place is hidden, the conversations are private. In the field Boaz takes to heart the fate of a helpless foreign woman by speaking kindly to her ("May your recompense be complete from the Lord. . . . under whose wings you have come to take refuge," 2:12). On the threshing floor Ruth takes a bold initiative by pointing out to Boaz where his duties lie ("spread your wings over your servant for you are a redeemer," 3:9). Boaz in turn becomes the obedient responder by repeating Ruth's earlier phrase to Naomi ("All that you say I will do," 3:11).

Empty House
(Ruth 1)

Who does not remember Ruth? Had we forgotten or misplaced most of the characters in the Bible, we should still remember her. Ruth, who gently walks from Moab to Bethlehem behind Naomi, who charmingly bends behind the harvesters, whose romance with Boaz ends in the start of a happy family. If we imagine Ruth in color, she comes in pastels. Her face unlined, her cloak unrumpled, she glides through the difficulties with which life faces her. The story is often called a peaceful idyll.

If we take a close look at the story we notice that peace and idyllic grace are rather far to seek in this tale. The first sentence of the book places it in the days of the Judges. No matter in what time the book was composed, the storytellers made its setting a time which more than any period in Israel's turbulent history was a time full of turmoil. Always at war or under threat of war, without constancy in political and religious leadership, the people were only at the threshold of being a nation. The book of Judges ends with the sentence that everyone "did what was right in their own eyes."

To underline the difficulties which would be an expected result of such a period, the story opens with a famine. We are today, perhaps more than ever before, aware of what that word means through the exposure to events in Africa. The story begins then with horror stalking the background. Into this situation a family is introduced, parents and two sons, who in seeking a future elsewhere than at home in Judah settle in Moab. First all seems to go well as they put down roots; the children marry and the future again contains the promise of life. But this family's history ends in loss and deprivation. At the end of a few sentences we find the woman Naomi, bereft of offspring and therefore of support, ready to go back home. "So she arose with her daughters-in-law and returned from Moab's fields" (6).

Of peace and idylls we hear little in the words of this widow to the two widows at her side: "Return my daughters," she pleads, "why should you go with me? Have I yet sons in my womb who may serve you as husbands? Return, please, my daughters, go; for I am too old to belong to a man. For said I 'there is for me hope,' yea belonged I this night to a man and even bore sons, would you wait for them until they grew up, would you restrain yourselves from belonging to a man?" (12–13).

So Naomi looks at herself, empty belly and all, and sees a lost cause with a future full of only ridiculous possibilities. One of the young women sees that Naomi is right and obediently returns home. One stays; stubborn and free in her own sense of who she is, to whom she belongs, sure in her own choice of what is good and kind. Stop, she says, do not ask me any longer to leave you, "to turn from following you;/for where you go, I go;/where you sleep, I sleep;/your people my people,/your God my God./Where you die, I die/and there I will be buried" (16–17).

Thus Ruth forms her unlikely alliance. Ruth knows that her choice means she has joined weakness to weakness, death to death. Like women today in our culture, she is conditioned to seek community anywhere but with another woman. Besides Naomi's voice her own instincts must have cried to her not to do such a foolish thing. She has every excuse, every justification to go back to the world that is familiar.

By Naomi, Ruth's alliance is not gratefully received. The text records that she stops speaking to her, and when they arrive in Bethlehem, she does not acknowledge Ruth's existence. "Do not call me Naomi," she cries to the neighbors, "call me Mara [or in a descriptive translation: Do not call me Sweetie, call me rather Sourpuss]. For the Almighty has shown me great bitterness. Full did I go, empty the Lord has caused me to return; why would you call me Sweetie? For the Lord has spoken against me and the Almighty has done me injury" (20–21). So she unloads all her grievance against God, and is not willing to believe that Ruth's presence is a sign of hope.

It is the storyteller who sounds the first note of hope with the phrase "they entered Bethlehem at the beginning of the barley harvest" (22). A first movement toward life is made here; harvest as a sign of abundance and fertility opposes the prevalence of death in the opening lines.

Guideposts

The story opens with an undercurrent of irony and an implied play on words, thus setting the tone for what is to follow. Certain words will be used for puns, others will be repeated, sometimes in a variety of meanings to point to the breadth of a concept. The narrator is especially skilled at setting up contrasting themes. The opening words sound plain, but for the careful listener there is ironic contrast in the phrases.

"It happened in the days that the Judges judged," is a time indication which sounds safe enough: those in office are doing their appointed work. But anyone who knows their history knows that next to infrequent periods of peace this was a time of turmoil and uncertainty, of broken promises and the threat of war.

Next we hear that "there was a famine in the land and a man from Bethlehem...." Bethlehem in Hebrew means "house of bread." Just in this particular place there is a lack of bread. Later in this section, the word *bread* is used when a reversal of the situation is reported: "the Lord had ... given them food." The word for food here is literally "bread" (*lehem* in Hebrew), a word used for the literal substance "bread" as well as generally for "sustenance and food."

The preacher can use these considerations to help draw people into the sermon. As on the face of it the house of bread, under just rule, should be the last place for a famine, so our world, full of supplies, should be the last place for shortage of food. While the current rulers rule they do not manage to keep the threat of famine and the plague of war at bay. Hunger and violence devour the people. The time in which Ruth is placed is not so unlike our time.

There is, however, something more going on in this story than a lack of supplies to keep people alive, a lack which is remedied anyway before the story is in full swing. For the person in the center, Naomi, there is a lack of life and hope for the future. The company of her sons' wives does not provide her with comfort. Their weakness only serves to emphasize her own weakness, their loss her loss, their lack of hope her lack of hope. "Return, my daughters," she urges, "return."

Of the three of them Naomi seems to know exactly what she is doing. She is on her way to the past; her house of bread is empty; the only things that remain there are the memories of the past, the beloved voices and faces of the dead. She refuses to see things as more rosy than they are. She requests of her daughters-in-law that they do the same thing that she is doing: to go back home, to return to the past. Their house of bread may even hold a new promise of life: "May the Lord grant you rest [i.e., a home] each in her husband's house" (9). A new household may yet arise upon the wreckage of the past. Naomi speaks to Orpah and Ruth on the threshold as it were; there are two ways to go and she points them in the right direction: Return, my daughters.

The word *return* is handled with deftness and shows how the narrator plays with opposites. At Naomi's request that they "return," the two women from Moab reply with the same verb: "No, with you we will return to your people" (10). In this reply the word has the opposite meaning from that which Naomi gave it. Naomi is returning home, the daughters-in-law would be going to a strange country. Naomi turns the word around to its original meaning of "to go back home" and so implores the women once more. After Orpah obeys, Naomi points out to Ruth that her sister has done the sensible thing, and wouldn't it be wise for her, Ruth, to do the same: "Look, your sister has returned to her people and her God, return after your sister" (15).

Ruth then, in her refusal of Naomi's request, gives the word *return* a deeper meaning. Going back home would mean for Ruth that she would abandon the weakest person around her. "Do not entreat me to leave you/to (re)turn from following you ..." (16). Ruth hears another voice than the voice of reason, she hears the voice of compassion and love. She hears the need of her weak neighbor speaking louder than any other voice.

There is a rich source for preaching ideas in the word *return* and the way it is employed in the text. The call to return sounds loud and clear to everyone, today as it did then. The subject of "return" can be manifold; from the "good old days," to traditional ways of worship, to familiar ideas about our faith and God, from our communal past to our individual past. One of these could become the focus of the sermon, whichever is most alive in the congregation and the preacher's mind. It should be made clear, however, that there is nothing necessarily wrong with tradition and established ways of doing things.

Once this has been pointed out the thought can be introduced that traditions become wrong if they rule us. If we hear only the voice of the past and stare in the direction of the past, of the "home" we have left, we may become "unfit for the kingdom of God." The call to go and to leave resounds through the Bible. Ruth has grasped what it may mean to become a part of a faith that is called a "way." She, the nonbeliever, shows Naomi and us that in showing kindness to others we show God's kindness to us; that in being loyal to others, we show God's loyalty to us; that in taking risks with each other we show the risk God takes with us.

Ruth has committed herself with her words to abiding in an empty house. Naomi again makes no bones about it when they arrive in Bethlehem: "full I went, empty the Lord has caused me to return" (21). How little the presence of Ruth comforts her is made clear. The only discernible impact of Ruth on Naomi is that she initially silences her. God receives the full load of her bitterness. Then the narrator intervenes to conclude this first episode and twice more uses the word *re-*

turn: "So Naomi returned and Ruth, ... who returned from Moab ..." (22). Now, in reality it can be said only of Naomi that she returned, since Ruth, as far as we know, has never been to Judah. Surely, in regard to Ruth the verb is here an awkward one! Yet the verb is the same that is used in the Bible of conversion, the turn to God which is so often demanded of God's people. Ruth truly made such a decisive turn.

The clear structure of the chapter can be used in organizing the sermon. Vss. 1–7, as the introduction, provide the background and set the scene for the women on the road. Vss. 8–18, the major unit, record crucial conversation between the main protagonists. Vss. 19–22 present the conclusion, beinging the scene of activity back to Bethlehem. The loneliness and emptiness of Naomi are emphasized in the introduction and the conclusion, with this difference: in the conclusion the narrator adds a double note of hope by mentioning the "return" of Ruth and by noting that the arrival in Bethlehem took place at "the beginning of the barley harvest" (22).

Instead of a famine there is now a harvest in the house of bread. This note points to the fact that in the story a reality is at work other than that which can be readily perceived. Ruth may think that she is on her way to a small village with little prospects for her future; in reality she is on the way to a place that will become the birthplace of kings and prophets. In reality she provides a vital link in the line to Jesus Christ.

The Ruth story shows us something vital about God and about what may happen if people, without guarantees, are willing to ally themselves to this God. Naomi's words to Ruth about the God of Israel give little reason for hope. Yet Ruth allies herself to this God with her words "your God my God" and thereby puts her hope in this God. She may have heard that the God of Israel is primarily concerned with the interests of those who are bereft of the vitality and power to survive. She has yet to be given proof of this concern, but she is willing to hope, hope that indeed there will be bread in Bethlehem. In so doing she shows those who came after her, no less than did Abraham (Gen 12:1–4), what it means to act on faith.

The story of Ruth is not a simple story of a good sister and a bad one, a good example and a bad example. Orpah, who goes back home, is not condemned; Ruth is far more than an example. She who seemed to choose a closed future instead made a choice which opened the future to the divine possibility of life. For God chose what is foolish in the world to shame the wise, and what is weak in the world to shame the strong. Out of Bethlehem, the house of bread where famine reigned, the bread of life will be born that feeds and heals a broken world. Ruth chose for this God. We can only be grateful that she made her choice which turned out to be a choice for the life of the world; for her we give thanks to God.

Opening Play
(Ruth 2)

The small note of promise for the future which the narrator sounded at the end of chapter 1 is continued in this chapter. First we hear that Naomi has a relative in town, a wealthy man, related to her through her deceased husband Elimelech. In the text lines Ruth takes the initiative to provide for the household and suggests that she go gleaning behind the harvesters; in the opening of the first scene "she happened by chance" to be on the field of just this relative, Boaz. In the field Boaz notices her, and after the initial inquiries, an elaborate conversation follows between the two in which he shows her increasing kindness. First he gives her his own permission to glean in his field, which would have the effect of making it impossible for the overseer to send her away. He encourages her to help herself when she is thirsty, since he has told his servants not to harass her. (This particular comment gives one the impression that such harassment may have been fairly common.) Ruth, in her reply, observes a humble politeness in the face of his preference. Boaz is lavish, both with his praise and with his goods. He wishes God's blessing on her for her kind deed toward Naomi and gives her a share of food at mealtime. Lastly, he commands his workers to leave something extra for her so that she goes home with a sizeable load of grain and the leftovers from the meal (there were from thirty to fifty pounds in the ephah).

The episode closes with a conversation between the two women, once Ruth arrives at home. This conversation, as we have noted, contains crucial information about Boaz. In addition, it shows a significant mood change for Naomi. Her part in the conversation contains praise ("blessed be he by the Lord," vs. 20), hope ("he is one of our redeemers," vs. 20), and encouragement ("it is good . . . that you go out," vs. 22).

Although the tone of this part of the story is optimistic, an undercurrent of anxiety is maintained. When we hear that there is a kinsman of Elimelech, the prospects for the women rise. They rise even more when we find Ruth in the field at this very same kinsman, Boaz! Yet Boaz does not mention his relationship to Elimelech when he speaks with Ruth, and though he treats Ruth with great kindness, it is the kindness of a master toward a servant.

When Naomi mentions the fact that Boaz is a redeemer, it has a twofold effect. Since Boaz himself did not show awareness of this fact when he talked with Ruth, it throws a different light on the conversation. Did he know that he is a redeemer? If he knew of the relationship and its responsibilities (and surely he would?), then his words and actions do not seem to have gone far enough. The "extra" given to Ruth does not reach the level of what could be expected of a relative; a relative who is, moreover, one of the redeemers.

The revelation made by Naomi also draws attention to the future. What will happen next? Again hopes rise. But the narrator closes the chapter by calmly reporting that Ruth followed Naomi's advice until the end of the harvest, an innocuous remark which has the effect of increasing tension. Any delay on the part of Boaz makes his actions more tentative.

In the sermon one should make full use of these two opposite movements. Things seem to be going well, but are they? If chapter one portrays life at the threshold, at a time when big decisions are made, chapter two shows life as it continues after the big decisions. There is some good news, but also some not-so-good news, or news that could turn out to be bad. We do not know yet. At the close of the chapter things are still as they were when Naomi and Ruth arrived in Bethlehem.

Guideposts

Words for "gleaning" and "harvesting" are prevalent in this chapter and point to the promise of life which is the dominant tone. This tone stands in tension to the questioning humility which Ruth assumes toward Boaz and the mention of time passing without the "gleaning" of more than temporary benefits. On the surface all is abundance, but the shadow of death and deprivation still falls over the life of the two women.

As in the first chapter the narrator opens the episode with a man. Naomi who sees herself as empty and bereft of support is not as entirely without resources as she might think. There is a man in the picture after all. And not just any man! Boaz is a kinsman, who is a "man of wealth." (The Hebrew *'ish gibbor hayl* can probably best be translated "a man of substance.") The words used here occur frequently in connection with men who are heroes in battle, and connote strength, courage, diligence, and also wealth. They will be used in chapter three at a climactic moment in regard to Ruth, and the storyteller here anticipates that moment.

The good news about the man is not pursued. The subject abruptly changes to Ruth, who offers to do something about the needs of the household. Her tone is both polite and determined, in keeping with the character drawn for us in the first chapter. She mentions in her announcement to Naomi for the first time the words "to find favor in the eyes of." Each time Ruth speaks, until she returns from the field, she uses the same phrase. As these words take on shape in her continued use of them, we are at the end still left with the question "Will she find favor?" They are words which are assumed by her in her inferior position, as they are always used to address a person of higher status. In a way Ruth establishes herself firmly in this episode as someone who must rely on the goodwill, the grace, of those around her. She does this not only by her use of the words connected with favor but also by her emphasis on her identity. First she describes herself as a foreigner (vs. 10), and then as someone who does not even belong to anyone's servants (vs. 13). When Boaz first speaks to Ruth in the field, she uses the expression of finding favor in a slightly different way than when speaking to Naomi. In the former, it mainly indicated that she needed someone's permission to glean. When she asks Boaz, "Why have I found favor in your eyes?" (vs. 10), she is speaking to the master of the house who is taking notice of her. Below the polite words echoes the desperation of this woman who has no one to notice her and, if no one does, may die. When she speaks for the third time, she dares to let hope for the future enter in: "May I continue to find favor in your eyes" (vs. 13; RSV "You are most gracious to me").

The verb "to take notice" is used twice in a key position. It is used pointedly in Ruth's first reply to Boaz (vs. 10) and later in the chapter by Naomi, before she finds out where Ruth has worked. "Blessed be the man, who took notice of you," she says (vs. 19). This root implies a taking notice for a desired purpose and is used elsewhere at a climactic point in narrative (see for example Gen 37:32; 38:25). Together with the expression "to find favor in the eyes of," it points to the tentativeness of Ruth's hope and to the degree in which people depend on working "kindness" (*hesed*) to one another.

When Naomi speaks of "kindness," it is the second time that this word occurs in the story. Once she wished that God would provide kindness for her daughters-in-law, as they had done for her family and herself. Now, she calls the man blessed by the Lord "whose kindness has not forsaken the living or the dead!" (vs. 20). In the Hebrew it is unclear whether it is the kindness of Boaz or that of the Lord which is referred to here. The ambiguity may be deliberate. In any case, the distinction is not as important as the pattern of "kindness" itself. Ruth sets *hesed* in motion by not abandoning Naomi, and thus she shows the pattern of *hesed* as it is practiced by the God of Israel whose *hesed* is "from everlasting to everlasting" (Ps 103:17).

It is one of God's qualities to be "abounding in *hesed*" (e.g., Jonah 4:2; Exod 34:6; Ps 103:8). Although this quality of God is particularly pertinent to God's people Israel, the *hesed* of God is not limited to them alone, as is shown by Ruth 1:8 (see also Jonah, and Ps 117:1). *Hesed* from one person to another has been called the self-denying readiness of someone to be present on behalf of someone else. It is that extra-quality which exceeds what is merely one's duty.

The word *redeemer*, already mentioned as a key word for the understanding of this story, occurs here for the first time (vs. 20). We will explore this concept in greater detail in our discussion of the next chapters. Here it must suffice to point out that something more may be expected of Boaz than has been shown so far.

The episode in chapter 2 is neatly structured with an introduction and a conclusion, which form the framework for the main action in the field (vss. 1–2 and 18–23). Both of these units contain a conversation between Naomi and Ruth, with some contrasts: Ruth opens the first dialogue, Naomi the second one (vss. 2 and 19); instead of the passive, almost curt, "Go, my daughter" of vs. 2, the conclusion finds Naomi almost effusive.

One can divide the action in the field into three sections. There is first the appearance of Ruth, then of Boaz in Boaz' field. The inquiry of Boaz follows, with the reply of the overseer (we note that the overseer calls Ruth "the Moabitess, who returned," vs. 6). Then comes the main section of this unit which consists almost entirely of dialogue (vss. 8–13), in which the character of Boaz is introduced as kind and generous. Ruth, in character, speaks well and is tactfully modest. By emphasizing her lowly position she is also able to point to her lack and her bleak prospects. Finally, there is the conclusion of this scene with a description of the meal and the abundance of food with which Ruth returns to Naomi (vss. 14–17).

At the end of the chapter the narrator lets time pass quickly in one sentence. Since Naomi and Ruth arrived in Bethlehem at the beginning of the barley harvest, seven weeks or so pass in vs. 23. We notice also the mention of harvest as at the conclusion of chapter one. This time the mention is of the end not the beginning of a harvest. This ending concludes a particular part of the drama. Something new must now take place so that events can move on.

All of the qualities of life emphasized in this chapter, as exemplified by "to find favor," "kindness," and "redeem," are those qualities which are necessary if the community of Ruth and Naomi is to become anything more than two isolated individuals who have become allies. A sermon could take as a focus the community of believers and what the pattern of life is that it should reflect, if it is to be a true community. A decision for community has been made in the book. What will enable the people in this story to live in a community? Ruth acts as an enabler in many ways. Such enablers are needed to shape community. The word *community* is frequently overused in our culture. What is the difference between an institution and a community? One can use the church as an example of an institution in which the decision for community has been made. If true community is created by the quality called "kindness" in the Bible, then how may this apply to the church and to a particular congregation? Community as it is created in the book of Ruth shows the far-reaching consequences of community. The effects of this once-upon-a-time, far away community are today felt all over the world.

The main theme of the chapter is what Campbell calls the "plus" factor (Campbell, p. 110). It is not enough that people do merely what is their obvious duty to one another. In chapter one it was not enough that Naomi would be accompanied on the road for a little ways. She needed company for life. This part of the story shows that it may not be enough to be kind, thoughtful, and pious (as Boaz is to Ruth), for at the end of the episode the continued life of the two women still hangs in the balance. Something extra is needed, the something extra that Ruth shows by going out and providing for her household. The "plus" factor goes to the heart of what the faith of Israel is all about. It is what *hesed* points to; it is what is consistently shown to the people by their God.

God shows this "plus" factor in not abandoning people, in being present on their behalf; in being present not only for one people but in them for the whole world. Immanuel, God-with-us as shown in Christ, is God's "plus" factor to us.

Whether all the people will show the pattern of *hesed* is not yet answered in chapter two. We have to wait and see how things develop.

A Call
(Ruth 3)

Chapter three presents the pivotal episode of the story. As in chapter two the main action is framed by a conversation between Naomi and Ruth. Naomi has now become fully awake to the possibilities that may lie ahead. What was only alluded to in her closing speech of the previous chapter here becomes specific.

In the first two lines Naomi makes clear reference to

Boaz' possible place in their future. With the word *home* she already once indicated marriage when she made her wish for Orpah and Ruth that the Lord might grant them "to find a home, each of you in the house of her husband" (1:9). At this point she admits her own responsibility in finding such a place for Ruth. Immediately Boaz comes to mind, and she refers to Boaz with a term almost identical to the one with which Boaz was introduced in chapter two, *kinsman*. Naomi then outlines for Ruth how she should go about the night's enterprise, giving her precise instructions. Ruth simply says that she will do all that Naomi tells her and is on her way to the threshing floor. As she has been instructed she lies at the feet of Boaz, whose "heart was merry" (vs. 7), indicating a sense of well-being and inebriation. Eventually, the man moves in his sleep and wakes up at the touch of something unfamiliar. Ruth identifies herself in the proper mode as "Ruth, your servant." With her next words she throws Boaz a curve and departs from the path so carefully laid out by Naomi. Naomi had told her that once she had positioned herself at Boaz' feet she should wait on his instructions, for "he will tell you what you should do" (vs. 4). Ruth does not wait until Boaz tells her what to do. Instead she tells him to "spread your wings over your servant, for you are a redeemer" (vs. 9; RSV "spread your skirt over your maidservant, for you are next of kin").

To these words, tantamount to a marriage proposal, Boaz gives a reply which is positive and full of praise for Ruth. The only proviso made is that someone else has redemption rights before him and needs to be brought into the picture. His elaborate and courteous speech echoes his earlier speeches when he met Ruth for the first time. He then exercises the same type of care for her, as he did earlier, by asking her to stay, yet making her leave before the morning has fully dawned to prevent a possible scandal. Before she leaves he lavishes gifts on her, to show his goodwill and generosity.

The chapter closes with Ruth's arrival at home and a final conversation between Naomi and Ruth. Both women speak their last words in the story, and these are words full of hope for the immediate future. Ruth comes to Naomi "not empty" (vs. 17), and Naomi's counsel ends with the word "today" (vs. 18).

All has not yet ended well but the scales are tipping in favor of a successful outcome. Naomi takes the initiative in the dialogue and gives Ruth her advice and fiat for what must have been a risky expedition. There is no hesitation on the part of Ruth, who shows the same determination that she has shown throughout the narrative. Indeed, in this chapter above all she gives evidence that she is willing to provide the one thing more, the extra, that is necessary for the events to move in the desired direction. Instead of passively relying on Naomi's instructions and waiting for Boaz to tell her what to do, she confronts him directly with his responsibilities for the *hesed* life and thus for the last time goes beyond what is strictly required of her. She has then indeed done all that is possible and in the narrative disappears from the center of the stage.

This part of our story has something of the burlesque about it. In preaching one should take advantage of this touch. We see here what Frederick Buechner has called "the Gospel as comedy" at work. There is little solemnity surrounding the scene on the threshing floor. Here are the two women plotting their next move. Naomi finally sees their chance and on her advice Ruth proceeds on her expedition to the threshing floor; decked out in her Sunday best and smelling of the latest in seductive scents she fumbles around in the dark to lie down at tipsy Boaz' feet. In her humanity she is yet like all those with whom God chooses to be involved. It is in these human circumstances that her words receive the power to move the story to its end. It is especially here, on the threshing floor, that we see the life of *hesed* at work. It is into this humanity that God descends to be with us.

We can look at this scene with the recognition that reality has more than one dimension. There are the obvious events which may consist of no more than an unconventional manner of one person seeking support from another. Underneath this surface there is the reality of life overcoming death in the story, of the need to fill Naomi's emptiness. Directly related to this is the reality of the future birth of Israel's greatest king, David. And, finally, there is the reality of the God who promises presence, the God-with-us, discernible in this slightly ridiculous couple.

Guideposts

The key words in this episode give evidence of the different levels of reality. When Naomi addresses Ruth, she speaks of a "home," as she had done earlier (1:9). Only then she wished that the Lord might find this home for Orpah and Ruth. Now she is aware that pious wishes of that sort seek their fulfillment in human activity.

In her directions to Ruth she uses a phrase which will be repeated twice with a slight variation. Naomi advises Ruth that once she has found Boaz, "he will tell you what to do." Ruth then replies with "all that you say I will do" (vs. 5). When she makes her bold proposal to Boaz he replies, "all that you say I will do" (vs. 11; RSV "I will do for you all that you ask"). By repeating this phrase once more, this time by the mouth of Boaz, the narrator brings out the irony of this response which follows on Ruth's not doing quite what Naomi told her to do.

In vs. 9 the Hebrew expression used can be translated with "spreading the mantle or skirt" and is elsewhere related to marriage customs (Deut 22:30; 27:20; and Ezek 16:8, for example). The RSV reads the phrase accordingly: "spread your skirt over your maidservant." It is very likely that Ruth with these words makes a marriage proposal. At the same time something more profound is indicated. The word usually translated "skirt" in the sentence means basically "wing." As such it occurred in chapter two when Boaz wished for Ruth the recompense from the Lord "under whose wings you have come to take refuge" (2:12). Wings in the Bible are a symbol of protection and power. We are not unfamiliar with this symbol when we speak of people taking someone "under their wing." Israel expects to be protected under God's wings. Hence the psalmist prays, "Keep me as the apple of your eye/hide me in the shadow of your wings" (Ps 17:8), and, "Let me dwell in your tent forever/Oh, to be safe under the shelter of your wings" (Ps 61:4). Jesus uses this image when he cries over Jerusalem, "How often would I have gathered your children together as a hen gathers her brood under her wings" (Matt 23:37). Boaz' pious wish for Ruth made in the field is supported by a solid tradition which sees God as the protector of Israel. Ruth in her turn makes Boaz directly responsible for the actual protecting which is necessary for herself and Naomi. She is perhaps not unacquainted with the emptiness of many pious wishes. Neither is she unacquainted with the task of protecting someone. She has throughout taken to heart the deprivation of another. She took on Naomi's empty life and has made it her business to make that life full. She has acted on the redeemer's task without the sanctions of the community and now makes her request of Boaz, authentically calling him to the same task to which he was appointed by community custom, "for," she says, "you are a redeemer."

If we translate the Hebrew term *kanaf* with "skirt," we have not only robbed Ruth of her pun but deprived the text of an essential part of its meaning. Here once more the narrator points to the correspondence between human activity and divine activity; the divine protection has to be brought into active operation through Boaz. Just as Ruth could not send Naomi on her way back to Judah with God's blessing but instead became God's blessing to Naomi, so Ruth asks at this moment that Boaz do the same. In so doing she calls on him as a redeemer. We have already said a few words about this concept and will have some more to say in our discussion of the next chapter. Let us here emphasize that she calls thereby on his responsibility as a member of clan or tribe to protect those who are without the power to protect themselves. Whether connected with property or release from slavery, redeemers are to function on behalf of persons and their property within the circle of the larger family; they are to take responsibility for the unfortunate and stand as their supporters and advocates. They are to embody the basic principle of caring responsibility for those who may not have justice done for them by the unscrupulous, or even by the person who lives by the letter of the law (Campbell, p. 136).

In this story the redemption practice is combined with that of so-called Levirate marriage, for which the basic principles are very much the same. In Levirate (from the Latin *levir* meaning brother-in-law) marriage a member of the immediate family marries the widow of a deceased family member who died childless. Only in Ruth are redemption practice and Levirate marriage associated, but this connection is a logical one. In Levirate marriage there is certainly a

concern for producing offspring, but there is also concern for
the care of the widow, and of course these concerns are not
separate.

Both of the practices, redemption and Levirate marriage,
belong to ancient Israel. Yet neither should seem far re-
moved from us as far as the supporting principles are concerned. Indeed, God became responsible for this unfortunate
world and is thus called a redeemer. That we should reflect a
pattern of responsibility toward one another is certainly not
alien to the Christian faith. Not only is this quality demanded of us in our communal life; we may also demand it
of each other; we may count on someone to make God's protection real to us.

In our story Ruth's choice for Naomi makes it possible for
Boaz to choose. As indeed he does. His words to her are filled
with praise. He calls her "blessed" and recounts her deed of
coming to him as a deed of *hesed*. Thirdly he calls her a
"woman of worth," and in so doing uses the very same words
by which he himself was introduced in chapter two, as a *'ish-
hayl*. Here obviously no wealth is implied, but certainly the
other meanings of *hayl* are valid—courage, strength, and diligence. "Valiant" might convey most accurately what the Hebrew intends here. Ruth is valiant in her choices, which are
not made because others dictate them to her. She knows
what it means to have allied herself to the God of the Presence, the God of Israel; it involves what Paul centuries later
will call the "freedom to be servants of one another through
love" (Gal. 5:13).

Then the narrator injects a last surprise by the introduction of one who has rights of redemption before Boaz. Boaz
takes an oath on it that he himself will do the job if the one
"who is closer in line" is not able to do it (vs. 13). His words
resound with the term *redeem*. He then instructs Ruth to lie
down. Words for "lying down" come thick and fast in this
episode. Rather than indicating that more took place than a
simple lying down, we should probably understand these
verbs as anticipatory to the next chapter. The verbs are
meant to call up images of sexuality and fertility but only
insofar as these images anticipate what will take place in the
final episode.

A final significant expression is used by Ruth when she

arrives at Naomi's with her full load of grain and reports
that Boaz had said, "You must not go back empty-handed to
your mother-in-law (vs. 17). Naomi's emptiness about which
she cried her bitter complaint earlier in the story is here already symbolically filled.

We mentioned in the Introduction to the book of Ruth
how chapters two and three both parallel and contrast each
other. They are constructed along the same lines: a conversation between Naomi and Ruth brackets the main episode
which takes place on the threshing floor. We notice, in contrast, how in chapter three the narrator leaves out introductory and concluding remarks and the conversation begins
and ends the episode. Naomi's instructions are detailed to
show her change of mood and willingness to participate completely in the plan. Ruth's reply is brief and significant.

The lines which serve to introduce the major scene (vss.
6–7) move quickly over what must have taken some time and
presented some difficulty. We notice the thick sequence of
verbs in vs. 7: "Ate . . . drank, . . . was merry, went to lie
down . . . she came . . . uncovered . . . and lay down." The
focus is on the moment when Ruth is discovered and on the
words that are spoken by each of the actors. This is the only
time that Boaz and Ruth converse while alone. The cheer-
leaders of the story are gone, which makes the conversation
all the more significant and powerful. Here they have no one
to show their goodwill, their humility, their *hesed* to but one
another. The words of Boaz, though satisfactory in the extreme, contain the one surprise which prevents the tension of
the story from slackening entirely. We still have to see how
Boaz will handle this with the redeemer who is closer in line.
The scene then concludes with the passing of the time until it
is almost light and with the last show of generosity on Boaz'
part. It is psychologically significant that Boaz asks her to
stay, for he could of course have sent her on her way home
immediately. If we believe that the story intends to convey
sexual intimacy then the reasons for his asking her to stay
are obvious. If we take another interpretation then his request to stay becomes, with his handing out of more provi-
sions, one final act of kindness. Boaz is beginning to show
that he understands what the "plus" factor consists of. Ruth
must have experienced great tension and anxiety as she

waited for Boaz to wake up. Though their conversation will
have set her mind at rest, he wants to make sure that she
understands his goodwill toward her and her family. He will
take care of the matter, as Naomi predicts later, but not in
any way that is improper and against Israelite custom.
Within this framework cleverness is certainly allowed, as
will be shown in chapter four, but not premature sexual intimacy with an unprotected young woman.

Boaz shows the same kind of consideration by sending her
home before people could see her. So Ruth arrives home and
the two women's last conversation is recorded, Naomi ending with the hopeful word *today*. She has come a long way
from the lonely Moab-Judah road where the only effect Ruth
had on her was to silence her.

A possible focus for a sermon is the theme of redemption.
When we call God our redeemer we believe with Israel that
God has taken on the responsibility for our helpless, powerless state and has restored us to the freedom and ability to
act and participate in the work of redemption for the world.

To participate means to be responsible with God for the
life of the creation, to spread our wings over the creation,
and in Christ we Gentiles may share this responsibility. The
question is whether we are ready to participate and to be
responsible for one another's welfare, and not only for one
another but especially for the well-being, the *shalom*, of those
who lack power, who suffer injustice. If in Christ we are set
free to become servants of one another through love, then we
are indeed responsible. Protection may be demanded of us,
as it was demanded of Boaz by Ruth of Moab. One last significant note may be that here the non-Israelite, a nonbeliever,
calls the believer to the task. She who could not have known
much about precise Israelite custom makes the Israelite
aware of his choices. So it may be for us that those who are
"not in the know" call us to the task of responsibility.

Full House
(Ruth 4)

The question as to whether Boaz will go the full measure
of his responsibility is not left in doubt for long. The next
morning sees him in full swing at the city gate, where cus-
tomarily such matters would be settled. Boaz waits until the

redeemer who is closer in line comes by; he invites him to sit down and proceeds to put the business before him. We find out that Naomi actually has property. It is not clear whether she herself was unaware of this fact, or whether she knew and was powerless to do much about the property until someone redeemed it. Boaz sounds businesslike and so does his coredeemer when he replies that he will do the job.

Boaz then informs him that Ruth is a part of any transaction that is to be made, upon which the redeemer takes back his consent and leaves the way open for Boaz. Boaz shows himself to be a clever manipulator in this episode. He holds the information concerning Ruth back until the redeemer has consented so that the acquiring of Ruth becomes an item in itself. Because of this way of presenting the case the other redeemer clearly sees all of the disadvantages and no advantages, so he leaves it to Boaz to fulfill the responsibility.

The narrator then interrupts the flow of the story with an explanation about the custom of removing the shoe. Unfortunately this explanation has the effect of obscuring further the already somewhat obscure details of the transaction. Boaz then calls the people to witness what he has in effect done, and a fairly elaborate witnessing report follows.

The scene switches to Naomi after the description of a longer period of time in one sentence (vs. 13). The spotlight is here on Naomi with the child in her lap and the community around her offering praise.

The very last section of the book consists of a genealogy which is commonly considered to be an appendix to the narrative, yet which does not necessarily clash with the impact of the story.

Guideposts

In outlining the structure of the chapter, the units may be broken down as follows: vss. 1–12 describe the transaction at the city gate and the response of those who witness the events; vss. 13–17 describe the birth of the child and the response of the neighbor women to the birth; vss. 18–22 form the genealogical appendix.

In vss. 1–12 words connected with redemption are key, as well as the noun for *name*, the names of people themselves and the word for house. In vss. 13–17 words for blessing and restoration predominate, as well as words for children (son, child, daughter-in-law) and fertility (conception, to bear). In this unit, too, names and naming are prominent. The entire book ends with a list of names. When one preaches from this part of Ruth the movement from the city gate to the circle around Boaz to the circle around Naomi should be kept in mind. In between there is the quick reference to the more private family environment in vs. 13; otherwise the emphasis of this chapter is on community. The genealogical appendix is not out of tune with this note since it recites the historical community.

Boaz and His Circle (vss. 1–12)

Chapter four of Ruth is unique in that it presents the description of an actual case of redemption. Furthermore, redemption and the custom of so-called Levirate marriage are here combined and Ruth is the only available material in which this combination is found.

The main legal material which deals with redemption is found in Lev 25:25; 27:9–33. The particular cases involving redemption may have to do with property, slavery, restitution, and acting as the avenger for a committed crime. Illustrations of the first and last cases can be found in Jer 32:6–25 and 2 Sam 14. From both the law codes and the narrative material, we can deduce a general principle which guided the practice of redemption: the stronger should take responsibility for the weaker (see above, p. 9).

That Levirate marriage is an issue in Ruth is clear from Naomi's speech to Orpah and Ruth in the first chapter. When she says, "Have I yet sons in my belly who might serve you as husbands?" the thought of this type of marriage informs her words. Naomi raises, rather sarcastically, the possibility of her giving birth to additional sons who might marry her daughters-in-law.

The main legal text in Deut 25:5–10 prescribes that a widow shall have the right of becoming a wife and mother with her deceased husband's brother. This practice is not unique to Israel and existed elsewhere in the ancient Near East. No doubt it was intended in first instance to protect against the threat of depopulation. In Deuteronomy, the practice is described as a right on the part of the woman, a duty on the part of the man, and the text includes a negative judgment on the man who is unwilling to respond positively. Gen 38 illustrates this last point very well. In this story which centers around Tamar, Judah, her father-in-law, is not living up to his responsibility in providing Tamar with an appropriate husband. In the end it is Judah himself who unknowingly fulfills the responsibility. The circle of those who were expected to assume responsibility for the widow was at one time probably quite large; certainly larger than that of brothers living in the same house. The story of Ruth witnesses to this extended circle as well.

As we observed earlier, the principle which guides both the custom of redemption and that of Levirate marriage can be described as the same: the care of the unfortunate by those who are in position to do so. In Ruth we see this guiding principle at work. It could be that the narrator has Boaz combine customs of redemption and Levirate marriage in one stroke. Where two customs would fit so eminently together no objections would be raised. Unfortunately, the scene at the city gate raises a number of questions. It is clear that neither redemption nor Levirate marriage was reserved for blood brothers. It is not clear what principle established the line of responsible people. Nor is it clear what exactly happened at the shoe exchange, though it is clear that no negative judgment is attached to it (in contrast to Deut 25). (For a list of unanswered problems in Ruth 4 see Campbell, pp. 157–61.) Regardless of the uncertainty with which we are left, the object of the actions is clear: an empty house needs to be filled. The storyteller expertly handles words for buying, acquiring, and redeeming. In addition, the names of all the people who have any stake in the matter occur. On the other hand, the redeemer closest in line is not named. Boaz uses a phrase for him which is probably best translated "so-and-so" (RSV "friend," vs. 1). This device works well. It would have been a distraction to introduce a new character at this stage of the story, only to take him immediately off the stage. Also, though the near-redeemer receives no negative judgment, he yet remains name-less, an indication that he is power-less since he does not exercise his power. Other names figure emphatically— the names of the living, Boaz, Naomi, and Ruth, but also

the names of the dead (identified as such in vs. 5),
Elimelech, Chilyon, and Mahlon.

The near-redeemer in the story functions only as a foil for
Boaz and his actions. In contrast to this no-name, the phrase
"name of the dead" is mentioned three times (in vss. 5 and 10
with the verb "to be perpetuated," in vs. 10 with the expression "not to be cut off"), and all the dead males in the family
occur here by name. The witnesses add to this list of names,
and also wish for Boaz "to bestow a name," in other words to
produce offspring. Life is here winning out over death and all
the references to names and housebuilding witness to this
fact.

Besides the names of traditional ancestors the witnesses
around Boaz bring other names to the fore which are worth
our attention. Rachel is well remembered for her difficulties
in childbearing, and she was certainly one who built the
house of Israel against great odds. Tamar had to resort to
tricking her father-in-law into sexual intimacy for her to participate in the continuation of the house. Since the outcome
for Rachel and Tamar was successful, the mention of these
two women points in a positive way to a hitherto unnamed
negative factor, that Ruth might be barren. She was after all
married for ten years without offspring.

Besides these considerations, the mention of the names
has the effect of placing Ruth, the foreigner, firmly within
the history and tradition of her adoptive people. Her own
words "your people my people" of the first chapter have
come into full operation by this witness giving.

So the couple marries and produces a son. All has ended
well, and the story could have stopped here. There is something, however, that remains unsaid. So far, the stress has
been on the name of the dead men, on Boaz' name; even the
women ancestors that are mentioned are seen in the service
of "building the house." As Phyllis Trible has pointed out,
"the men make Ruth the means for achieving a male purpose" (p. 192). The only thing that concerns the actors up
until vs. 12 is that the name of the dead man live on, not that
the two widows would find protection and a new fulfilled
life. Though the two concerns cannot be so sharply divided, it
must be admitted that the repeated interest in vss. 1–12 is
directed more toward the dead males in Naomi's family, and

to Boaz himself, than to Ruth and Naomi. The storyteller does not leave the listener with unanswered questions, however, and the end of the story belongs to the community around Naomi, to their words of praise, and blessing, and name giving.

Naomi and Her Circle (vss. 13–17)

The women whose welcome had been bitterly refused by Naomi on her return to Bethlehem now speak their praise. "Blessed be the Lord," they say, "who has not withheld a redeemer from you today" (vs. 14; RSV "who has not left you this day without next of kin"). This is the last time that the word *redeemer* occurs and here the reference is blurred. Is it Boaz? Is it the child? Or is it perhaps God? It is after all God to whom they turn with praise now that all the human labors are in the past. While the antecedent is most likely the newborn child, especially in view of vs. 15, there is probably a deliberate ambiguity at work.

In vs. 15 the ambiguity disappears. The women are now talking about the child in words which are highly significant. For "restorer of life," the Hebrew has "one who causes life to return," and hereby the narrator picks up the thread that was once woven into the fabric of the story by the verb "to return" (see above, pp. 17–19). For the women the significance of the child is that it causes life to return to Naomi, she who returned from Moab empty. The story has come full circle when the women say, "A son has been born to Naomi" (17). Their attention is directed to the one who was bereft of children and now sits with the child in her lap.

Ruth, who went ignored on their entrance into Bethlehem, receives the strongest praise: "Your daughter-in-law who loves you has borne him, and she is better to you than seven sons!" (vs. 15). It is ironic to find this evaluation of Ruth in a story where so much hangs on the birth of a male child! The women then name the child, and the narrator reveals the final piece of information, that he became the grandfather of David.

The community that once was forbidden to give a name, names the newborn child. So we take leave of Ruth and Naomi, who are surrounded by promise for the future. Let the genealogy serve to underscore the stress on community as we find it in this chapter. A couple of isolated women are finally in the presence of community, past, present, and future.

The theme of redemption comes to its conclusion in this chapter. This theme holds the restoration of life and community within itself. An appropriate focus for a sermon could be vs. 14. It is God who is ultimately held responsible, and who is praised for not withholding the redeemer. The fruits of this redemption lie in the future, yet the attention is drawn to the present: "today."

The images of vss. 14–17 foreshadow the birth of Christ in whom life and community are restored. In Naomi's empty and isolated life the fullness of community has entered. There is the child, and there is Ruth, and there are the neighbor women. Names which convey the presence of people abound in this part of the story. The communion of saints, the cloud of witnesses is recorded here.

Our interest may be in our own name, as evidenced by the witnesses at the gate and by Boaz. Our presence and importance come first. The end of the story says otherwise. The Redeemer, the life restorer, stands in the center of the stage and with the Redeemer are the unfortunate, the bereft, powerless characters.

ESTHER

Introduction

More than many books in the Bible, Esther is surrounded by controversy and a host of problems. In this case the controversies center not so much on its date and origin as on its content. In the past the book's canonical status was long insecure, in both Judaism and Christianity. In the life of the church it is one of the least popular texts for preaching.

Much of the dislike toward Esther is summed up by the following comment: "a Christian minister . . . faithful to the context, . . . will not take a text from Esther; and if the leader of a church-school class shows any Christian discernment, he will not waste time trying to show that the heroes of the book are models of character, integrity, and piety" (B. W. Anderson in Moore (ed.), p. 140).

Date

Most scholars agree on a final editing of Esther some time in the second century B.C., although there is less agreement on the time of its origin. Moore gives a date between 400 and 114 B.C. as the extreme limits for first and final editions. (See Moore, *Esther*, pp. vii–ix for an overview.) Certainly, the book is post-exilic, even by its own designation. According to the text, the story is set at the court of Ahasuerus, who is commonly identified as the Persian king known in Greek as Xerxes, which would place the events around 475 B.C. The actual circumstances in which the book was finally edited and circulated may have been more like those of the time of Antiochus Epiphanes (175–163 B.C.), a time of severe oppression and persecution for the Jews. A book as this, with its clever intrigue and escape from death, would certainly gain in popularity in such times.

Opinions differ widely as to the origin of the story. Is it history, fiction; is there a pagan source for the Purim festival? Moore decides on the category of historical novel, with a story about Mordecai as its source. Much in his reasoning remains speculative. The fact that details of the Persian court are accurately presented, as well as the actual existence of names used in the Esther story, in itself proves nothing. Any good storyteller would make use of as many accurate details and realistic names as possible. It seems impossible to prove the existence of a Purim festival elsewhere. We know that the festival exists in Judaism and that Esther is directly related to the festival. We should not forget that Purim, a late winter celebration (February–March), is a time of high jinks and dress-up, a playful festival, for it may help us in gaining a better understanding of the text.

Like Ruth, Esther wandered around in the canon; sometimes it is placed following Lamentations, sometimes after Daniel, or, as in the Greek (Septuagint), after the Wisdom of Sirach; in the Christian versions Esther follows Nehemiah. A curiosity of this book is that the Greek text has six major additions which change the tone of the book toward greater religiosity. (The additions can be found in any edition of the Apocrypha.) A final note of interest is that Esther is the only book of the Hebrew Bible which is not represented among the Dead Sea Scrolls.

Content

It would be difficult to talk about the theology of a book which presents no discernible theology. This omission has not deterred people from ascribing a theology to it. Perhaps the most plausible of the suggestions is the proposal by Cohen that the book opposes a fatalistic view of reality: "Haman rests his hopes on chance, (the pur), but providence prevails. . . . Indeed in naming the holiday Purim, the full significance of the holiday is disclosed to us. Purim is the appellation of a problem; . . . do chance and determinism rule supreme in the universe, or does God?" (Abraham D. Cohen in Moore (ed.), p. 129).

Such an explanation, however, does little to alleviate the problems of the book. One of these is the seemingly strong nationalism which is not explicitly undergirded by religious convictions, combined with the bloodthirstiness of the last chapters. Obviously this book does not present one of the easiest texts for preaching, and Anderson's remark, quoted above, is only one of many made in similar vein by other scholars. Luther's dislike for the book is so well known and so often quoted that it need not be repeated here, were it not for the fact that one part of his comment deserves particular attention. Luther said about Esther and 2 Maccabees that he wished "they did not exist at all; for they *judaize* too greatly and have much pagan impropriety" (*Table Talk* xxiv). Precisely what Luther did not like may be what we should emphasize. Perhaps more than any other biblical book, Esther faces the church with its Jewish roots, with the meaning of Israel's survival, and with the issue of the church's relationship to Judaism and the Jews. It is all too easy for the church to spiritualize the meaning of the election of Israel into a general idea which then automatically is transferred to the church. In Esther we are faced with the concrete and continued existence of the people who are the children of God's covenant. Although I would hesitate to put Esther in the historical novel category, we should be careful not to rob the book of its historical ties. Esther is closely tied to the survival of a people caught in the providence of God. Esther is a folktale which should be viewed through the screen of a particular historical situation.

A strong resemblance of Esther to the exodus story has been noted by some scholars. Regardless of the merits of this particular theory, the comparison is significant. The exodus narrative is used as a paradigm by many liberation theologians. One might say that the exodus of Israel from Egypt has become *the* paradigm for liberation theology. The story of the exodus is that of a people who have experienced liberation, who have experienced God as taking sides with the downtrodden and the oppressed.

Esther, on the other hand, is the story of a people who are in the middle of the oppression experience, a people who somehow must deal with the fact that God's chosen are lead-

ing a life which they would not have chosen. If the story of
Esther indeed took its final shape during the reign of Antiochus Epiphanes the sight and sound of the oppressor dominated the days of the Jews. In such times, trickster stories
like the one of Esther take on crucial significance, somewhat
like the stories of Uncle Remus. How does one survive in
times when it is not apparent that God is on the side of the
oppressed? One of the ways of surviving is to tell the tale of
the trickster who outwits the powers in charge. Esther is
such a tale.

In an article written in 1977, Bruce William Jones emphasized the humor in Esther. He makes the assumption that "it
is easier to bear pain or subjugation if one can mock those in
authority or those responsible for the pain" (in Moore (ed.),
p. 438). I suggest that we state this assumption more
strongly: making fun of those in power makes pain bearable
for the oppressed group. I remember from the Second World
War the songs of mockery sung by my mother when we were
helpless in the power of Nazi Germany. After the war whole
collections of poetry and stories were published, which
showed this to have been a national pastime in The Nether-
lands. Mockery and ridicule of the oppressor may well be
essential for survival.

If we want to preach from this book we may have to look
in the direction indicated above. Esther, full of human
shrewdness and cunning against overpowering odds, has
something to teach us about the life of God's people *before*
the song of liberation is sung. It also has something to say to
our guilt in the face of centuries of persecution and hatred of
the Jewish people. In addition, if we see the main issue of
Esther to be the survival of the Jewish people, we are dealing
with a religious issue.

Literary Structure

The book can be divided as follows: introduction, providing the necessary background and setting the scene for the
events to come (chapters one and two); the main story, which
tells of Haman, his plot against the Jews and how he is foiled
(chapters two through seven); conclusion, which gives the
foundation for Purim (chapters eight and nine); postscript
(chapter 10).

The style of Esther relies on repetition and exaggeration for its effectiveness. At times, as in the pivotal chapter four, the style becomes more terse. Physical beauty of environment and people is repeatedly reported, as in the details of the royal splendor in chapter one, the beauty of the queen, and the beauty of Esther in chapter two. Below the surface of these descriptions moves the idea that it is not splendor and beauty which lend power. All the trappings of royalty cannot make Queen Vashti appear at the king's command. The best that his circle of advisors can come up with for the royal edict is that men will be boss in their own household (1:22)! It is in the end not Esther's beauty, though she is called beautiful, but her wisdom which saves her and her people. She is able to "find favor" in the eyes of those around her by her words and actions, as is emphasized when she is introduced in chapter two.

Nor do riches save one. Haman's riches, of which he boasts to those around him (5:11–12) only cause him to indulge in extravagant anger and lust for revenge. He consistently overreaches himself. The gallows, fifty cubits high, shows the measure of his bloated self-image. He himself will hang on the instrument of death intended for Mordecai, who will take his place at the king's court.

The characters in the story are introduced in a manner which allows for little surprise in what follows. The king is introduced as easily manipulated and impressionable and continues to behave this way; Mordecai is solicitous and has an ear to the ground; Haman is a vengeful tyrant. The only character which is developed through the story is that of Esther, who does not come into her own until chapter five following and who shows increasing skill in dealing with those who are in power. Those who have suggested that her character is built on the model of the sage may well be correct.

Purim is a feast and the feast theme is a central one in the book. It opens with a king's feast, which is unsuccessful, is followed by a king's feast for a queen (chapter two), and is contrasted with a feast given by a queen which is successful in what it set out to do (chapter seven). At the first feast a queen loses her crown, a crown which meant little more than enhancement of her beauty, at a feast which had little more as its goal than an ostentatious display of riches. At the feast given by Esther a queen gains, not a crown which she already had been granted, but the power which properly belongs to a crown, during a feast held for the purpose of outwitting the enemy.

At the first feast the king makes a request of the queen to which she responds negatively; at the feast given by Esther, the queen makes a request of the king to which he responds positively. There is a role reversal as well as a reversal of requests. What was trivial in the first chapter, the appearance of a beautiful woman, is crucial in the seventh chapter for the life of a people. The upshot of the request in chapter one is the empty declaration that men are "kings of the castle." An immediate result of the request in chapter seven is that Haman is "enthroned" on the gallows.

Although the style of the story is very different from that of Ruth, there is no less evidence of skill in writing and structure. The preacher can make full use of the story and its developments, drawing as many parallels between it and the contemporary situation as possible. On one level the book has as its subject the hatred and persecution of the Jews, on another it offers insight into the dynamics between any group of oppressors and oppressed.

Some chapters afford better opportunities for preaching than others. Chapters one and two, for example, can perhaps best be used as an introduction to a sermon on chapter three.

A King's Feast
(Esther 1)

A brief retelling of the story may be one way to draw the listeners into the focus of the sermon. Esther in some of the episodes has a "listen-to-this" flavor. The scene opens with Ahasuerus in charge of the household and the kingdom, busy giving a feast. Yes, that same king, you heard about him, the one who reigned in Susa over, . . . How many provinces did you say? I have it on the best authority that there were one hundred twenty-seven! Well, anyway, he gave the biggest party you have ever imagined. Anyone who was anyone was there, basking in the royal sunshine for days without number. When they were done, the king was not done, and continued throwing a party, this time for everyone who had not been invited the first time. You can imagine how they gawked, the beggars and burghers of Susa city, at all that white and blue, the silver, the marble and the gold; even the drinks were served in gold. They said the queen was at it too.

Then all the partying finally got to the king and he did something he probably would not have done if he had been entirely sober. He called the eunuchs to go to the harem and get Queen Vashti. "And remind her to put on her crown," he said. He thought that would really wow 'em, you see. But then the eunuchs came scurrying back and no queen. She said she couldn't be bothered, that she was too busy entertaining at her own party.

You may have seen people get angry, but I doubt that you have ever seen anything like the king when he heard this. He stomped around, purple in the face, threw his gold cup against a marble pillar, tore down some curtains, and when he finally could get his breath he shouted for his advisors. Seven of them there were, bowing and scraping and barely able to ask "what-do-you-want-O-Majesty-most-high," for fear that he would pick on one of them. The king said: Did you hear what Vashti said? Is that legal? Well now, that was a good question. If anyone dared to answer the truth, that whatever may be said about Vashti's manners she certainly had not acted against the law, the king could make him a scapegoat.

So there they stood, coughing and trying to hide their embarrassment, until one of them began to talk. He used just the right words, in long soothing sentences which avoided a direct answer as much as possible and yet managed to get to the heart of the matter. Imagine, he said, if the court gets word of what went on in here. If the queen won't do what her husband says, what about all the other women? They will feel free to treat their husbands like dirt. An example must be made, right here and now, of Vashti, and since you are the lawmaker, write it down as a law. Vashti cannot come near you again and you will give her crown to another woman. That will scare the women into behaving.

Well, that suited everyone, including the king, and royal messengers went out, all over the one hundred twenty-seven provinces, with letters in different languages to make it clearly understood how the king had dealt with Vashti and that from now on every husband would lay down the law in his own household. So there!

I have recast the story deliberately in a colloquial style, almost like a children's story. The contrast between the royal splendor and the royal edict is striking. King Ahasuerus the magnificent does little but show his lack of power by declaring the man of the house in charge. He cannot compel Vashti to appear before him for the moment so he forbids her to appear before him for ever.

The original story presents a series of vignettes. The double feast, first for the nobles, then for the people (vss. 1–4, 5–9); then the idea to make it all more beautiful yet by the presence of Queen Vashti, the royal command and Vashti's refusal, which causes a royal temper tantrum (vss. 10–12); subsequently the king goes to his advisors to help him sort this out (vss. 13–15); in reply comes Memuchan's speech, a masterpiece of evasion and manipulation. What has happened is not just a matter between husband and wife but will affect the entire court, no, the whole country. All the ladies at the court and elsewhere will surely follow suit (vss. 16–18); once he has his listeners in a receptive mood Memuchan gives concrete advice (vss. 19–20); this advice is followed by the king as is described in the last unit (vss. 21–22).

In the first subsections words for splendid accoutrements are piled on top of each other. The size of the kingdom is emphasized, the word *all* occurs a number of times to indicate the largesse of the king. There are seven eunuchs, seven advisors. And surrounded with all this splendor and good advice the king can do no more than forbid a woman to do what she did not want to do in the first place and utter the platitude that men rule the roost! What will these people think of next!

A King's Harem
(Esther 2)

That question is answered in the next chapter when the scene opens on a king who has sobered up and before he can think better of his former actions is given new advice. The queen will have to be replaced. What better way to proceed than by filling the harem so the king will be able to make a good choice? The words *best* and *beautiful* abound in this unit (vss. 1–4).

Before the action moves to the actual gathering of the young women, Mordecai and his family are introduced. The narrator is careful to give his tribal antecedents as well as his direct ancestry which will set him in direct opposition to Haman, the hated Agagite. With him is his cousin Esther, who is also his ward, as she is an orphan. Again we hear the word *beautiful*, this time in reference to Esther. Since Esther is as good a candidate for the royal harem as any young woman, we find her there in the next section (vss. 8–11). She is getting the beauty treatment which will help her to please the king and is living as a Gentile at the gentile court. Mordecai shows his continued care by inquiring after her daily.

The following unit slows the action again by describing the customs of the harem, the details of the beauty treatment, and the visit to the king. It is apparently no great exception for a woman not to be asked into the royal presence more than once.

Esther's turn comes and she is successful. The king makes her queen and takes to partying again. All is back to normal in the royal household (vss. 15–18).

Yet, all may not be as well as it seems. Twice we are told that Esther hides her nationality (vss. 10, 20) and the conclusion of the chapter tells of a plot against the king which is successfully intercepted by Mordecai, who hangs around the court, hears things, and acts as an informant (vss. 19–23). Although this unit has no immediate consequences, it is vital to the development of the story as will be seen.

Esther is described not only as beautiful but also as prudent. She is obedient to her guardian even when she is no longer under his direct supervision, and pays respectful attention to Hegai, the supervisor in the harem. Twice it is stated that she "found favor." More than beauty she has prudence and charm.

The chapter ends with a hanging. Another feast, another punishment, but the stakes are higher, the punishment more serious—shadows of events to come.

Seeds of Destruction
(Esther 3)

Enter Haman, the villain of the piece. In a strikingly jarring sentence the chapter opens with the king elevating Haman to a high position at the court. A logical followup to the end of chapter two would have been the awarding of Mordecai; instead the narrator reports the elevation of one whose house is from of old hostile to Israel (1 Sam 15). Moreover, the hostility is aggravated in this case since both Mordecai and Haman are descendants of the main protagonists in the hostile activities of the past: Mordecai is reportedly related to Saul, Haman to Agag, the Amalekite king.

Haman is placed so high that he receives the honor of having others prostrate themselves before him. Mordecai refuses to participate in this action for unstated reasons and the servants tell on him.

Supposedly Haman had not noticed the one exception before but now he does and is also made aware by the servants that Mordecai is a Jew. Haman is filled with fury and decides to go for the whole people instead of just for Mordecai alone. He manipulates the king into agreeing to a wholesale slaughter and the decrees go out in the first month that the destruction will take place in the twelfth month.

Guideposts

The chapter can be divided into smaller units. The first unit, vss. 1–2, opens with the rising at the court of Haman, who is purposefully introduced with his ancestry. It ends with Mordecai who refuses to lie down before Haman. The word *all* is a key word in the beginning of the chapter: "all the princes," "all the servants."

In the next unit an anonymous group of servants take over the main action. Servants and other groups as advisors or family members perform an important function in the story. They are the entourage, always around, ready to move the story on. Most of the time they are anonymous, some of the time they receive a name. Here, in any case, they perform the crucial role of passing on an essential piece of information to one of the main characters. This section (vss. 3–4) is full of words for speaking and telling: "the servants . . . said . . . they spoke . . . they told . . . he had told. . . ." They do indeed tell. Not only do they make Haman aware of the one insubordinate character, they also tell him his nationality as we find out from the next unit. As the king did earlier to Vashti's refusal, Haman reacts with extreme anger to

Mordecai's refusal. His anger exceeds that of the King in that he determines to go after an entire people, not just one individual, and sets out to destroy their life, not merely to trap them permanently in a lowly position. The verses repeat the name of Mordecai so that it seems to echo with the "o-ai" sound, an ominous prelude to the planned destruction.

Haman next prepares his plans. As others have pointed out, the logic of the Pur-casting is no longer known but certainly it must have been used to forecast a propitious day. The day is chosen and Haman goes to the king.

Vss. 8–11 show Haman to be a clever manipulator who plays on His Majesty's fear as well as his greed. He begins by an innocuous statement that there is a particular people who are "scattered and dispersed among the peoples in all the provinces" (vs. 8). There may have been a number of groups to which this statement could apply. Yet the opening words make it clear that these people are not a small group and they are not concentrated in one area; they are all over the place! Haman then goes on to point out that these people's "laws are different from all people." In one sense this is also true enough. Jews had their own dietary laws, their own speech; they may have dressed differently, and they kept their own religious calendar. But this much could probably be said of a number of other ethnic groups within a kingdom known for its tolerance in such matters. By using the word *laws* Haman introduces a fearful element into the picture, and he completes this by immediately adding that these people do not obey "the laws of the king." This last statement is as good as a lie, and he gives no illustration of its truth. To the ruler of the land it must have sounded something like this: there is a people around in the kingdom, all over the place as a matter of fact, who think that they are a law unto themselves!

Next, Haman plays on the natural greed of any ruler by offering money to do away with these people. The money offered amounts to an exorbitant sum, an indication of the way in which exaggeration is used in the book to allude to character. Haman is beginning to overreach himself. The last verse of this unit reads in the RSV: "And the king said to Haman, 'The money is given to you, the people also, to do with them as it seems good to you.'" In view of what precedes and what follows we should understand this sentence as hyperbole for

the king's acceptance of Haman's offer. Perhaps we should
read with Moore: "Well, it's your money, said the king to Haman, do what you like with the people." The concluding unit
(vss. 12–15) describes once more the royal apparatus at work
issuing royal decrees. Detailed instructions are given, and after the king has seen that everything will be done in order, he
and Haman sit down to seal the bargain with a drink. "But,"
so the chapter ends, "the city of Susa was perplexed."

Questions and Suggestions

Perplexity may well be what fills us after reading this
part of the story. There is much here that is not immediately
understandable. Why did Mordecai refuse to bow down?
Why did Haman get so angry that he wanted to kill off an
entire people, and, above all, why is the intended destruction
announced almost a year before it is to take place? As to the
latter, the text says, "so that the people would be ready on
that day." But surely they would not need this much notice?

There are several things going on here which we may best
understand from the point of the relationship of the oppressors and oppressed. Let us remember that the story may well
have taken its final shape during the days of severe persecution. Anyone in authority in such times is an oppressor, a
tyrant. The narrator of Esther takes pains to paint Haman as
one who fits the role well. Mordecai is a member of a perse-
cuted and despised people and he refuses to be polite to the
persecutor. From a psychological point of view this is infuri-
ating to the persecutor and so Haman's rage is fully understandable. There is also something laughable about it, as
there is about the rage of petty tyrants.

Retaliation in the form of group punishment is a common
tactic on the part of oppressors. And this is precisely the tactic Haman employs. The king is Haman's dupe. The simple-
ton gives in as soon as he perceives a threat to his authority
and hears the sound of coins clinking in the royal coffers. The
destruction of the Jews is announced in gruesome detail:
"destroy, slaughter, and annihilate, all the Jews, from boy to
old man, children and women." (vs. 13). A holocaust!

The advance notice has a double effect. To the enemy the
intent is to plan the destruction well and make the Jews go in
fear for their lives for the rest of the year. On the other hand

the Jews now also know and are put on their guard. In the meantime there is opportunity for some people to work out their counterplans.

Contemporary parallels to this part of the story are not far to seek. "There is one people ... different ... the laws ... they do not obey." The Jews have set themselves apart, they are different, they stick together, they are a law unto themselves. Who knows what they are plotting? They do not feel bound to the laws of the land. They do not accept the same authority we accept.

And so over two thousand years this people has been made a scapegoat for all manner of calamity that have befallen the world, from drought, to plague, to economic disasters. Until it ended in the mass graves of the extermination camps. By a clever fabrication of truth, half-truth, and outright lie Haman maneuvers the king into agreeing to the death of a whole people. Such hatred is always made up of a combination of truths and half-truths which together make a whole lie and together aim for destruction.

We, the Christian church, have played in regard to the Jews the part of Haman, or the king; either we wove the tissue of lies ourselves and plotted their destruction, or we allowed the destruction to take place until the tide of hatred became so strong that there was no stopping it. Haman shows us how the seed of destruction is sown.

Taking this hatred as a focus, a sermon could proceed to point to the necessity for eradicating this prejudice and all such prejudice according to the demands of the gospel. We are not arbiters of the fate of the Jews, who are, as they always have been, in God's presence. Insofar as we have been guilty of acting as their judges and persecutors we should approach Israel with repentance, and all the statements which the church makes should have repentance as their basis.

Difference on the part of any group tends to cause anger, of course, not only the difference created by the Jews. Refusal to conform, especially on the part of a dominated group, to the rules made by the ones who have the power is severely punished. Mordecai's refusal to bow is not just a refusal to pay respect to the enemy, it is also a refusal to conform. It is telling that Haman puts the nonconformism of the Jews as their first offense. The oppressed should play by the rules of

the oppressor and as soon as there are signs of this not being
the case this spells danger to the oppressor.

In the kingdom of God, given to us in Jesus Christ, there is
however a freedom which goes straight against our inclina-
tion to condemn nonconformism. In the kingdom each individual and each group keep their uniqueness and they are
not forced to conform to each other's presuppositions.

"There is a certain people" in the kingdom who first
taught about the God of love. For their unique presence let us
give thanks to God.

Who Knows
(Esther 4)

Chapter four is the pivotal chapter of the story. In it Esther is faced with the choice to mediate on behalf of her people, a choice she makes only after some difficulty. This is the
only part of the narrative which reports an interchange between Esther and Mordecai, albeit an interchange which is
directed by go-betweens. The servants have again a crucial
function in moving the story along.

On hearing the bad news Mordecai goes into loud public
mourning. Presumably he did not differ in this action from
his compatriots: "sack and ashes were the bed of many" (vs.
3). Yet, the place of his mourning is purposefully chosen,
close enough to the palace, so that Esther will surely hear
of it.

Esther does indeed receive the information and her first
response is to send Mordecai clothes. When Mordecai refuses
them she sends one of her own servants to find out the reason
for his behavior. Mordecai tells Hatak, Esther's servant, what
has happened and what will happen and sends the message
back that Esther should mediate on behalf of her people with
the king. Esther refuses since she has not received express
permission to come into the king's presence and there is mor-
tal danger when someone goes uninvited into the king's presence. Not only does she not have an invitation, she has not
had one for quite a while.

Hatak goes to Mordecai with Esther's refusal and
Mordecai makes a second attempt to persuade Esther to in-
tercede. By using a mixture of threat and promise he suc-
ceeds and Esther accepts. She asks her people to fast with

her and after the fast she will approach the king. The chapter ends with Mordecai's leaving the city square and presumably organizing the fast.

Guideposts

The chapter is full of coming and going. The movements of others are framed by those of Mordecai who approaches the palace in the first verse and leaves in the last. In the main section the major characters, Esther and Mordecai, stay in their place while messengers scurry back and forth carrying information.

Subdivisions are easy to make. The scene is set by Mordecai's placing himself in the city square at the entrance of Kingsgate which is the gate to the palace grounds. There he makes a commotion. These first verses are full of the sound of lamentation (vss. 1–3).

In vss. 4–6 the scene switches to Esther; from now on it will switch back and forth from Mordecai to Esther. She finds out from her servants what is going on but not why it is going on. She is frightened but we are not told why. It may be that her sense of propriety is offended. In any case, she sends clothes so he may cease what he is doing. Mordecai refuses and only then does Esther send a special person to find out why Mordecai is behaving in this way. Verbs of coming and going enclose this subunit: Esther's maids come in (vs. 4) and Hatak goes out (vs. 6).

The following verses report Mordecai's telling the whole story to Hatak (vss. 7–9), including the sum of money which Haman has promised to the king, and he gives Hatak a copy of the royal decree to show to Esther. The knowledge of the impending disaster and Mordecai's pleas by the mouth of Hatak will convince Esther to do the right thing. She has after all always obeyed him before. Verbs follow each other rapidly to give the impression of urgency: "to show Esther ... to tell her ... urge her to go ... to implore and beseech him" (vs. 9). The unit ends with Hatak's coming back to Esther and telling her Mordecai's words. We should probably think of this as a literal repetition of his words.

Esther sends Hatak back with a refusal (vss. 10–12). Although she does not say in so many words "I won't go," she points to the risks of the task. The risk is too great, as "all the people know." This subsection ends with the report of Esther's words to Mordecai. Here for the first time in the chapter the narrator directly reports speech, because at this crucial moment Esther's refusal needs to be repeated word for word.

Mordecai's reply is also directly quoted. He goes to the heart of the matter without ado: if it is a matter of risk, he points out, you are as much at risk by not entering the king's presence. This remark is followed by a somewhat obscure statement referring to "deliverance for the Jews from elsewhere" and we will return to this sentence. He ends his words by pointing to Esther's possible destiny. She may think that she has become a useless ornament in the harem; in reality it may be quite otherwise. The speech ends abruptly and we have to assume that it is reported to Esther (vss. 13–14).

The concluding verses (15–17) describe Esther's acceptance of the task with her call for a fast and fatalistic sounding words "If I perish, I perish." The verbs in this unit follow each other in rapid succession: "Go . . . gather . . . hold a fast . . . neither eat nor drink . . . I will fast . . . I will go." In view of the importance of the words for movement in the chapter the question is left open as to whether the movement will end in life or death.

Questions and Suggestions

This part of the story raises a number of questions. For example, why does Esther not know something which the whole empire knows? Why do Esther's maids tell her of Mordecai's behavior? Do they know that she is Jewish? If they do not know about the relationship then why tell her about Mordecai's mourning? What underlies Mordecai's words to Esther? Are there references to divine intervention and guidance here? Why is there such a glaring absence of the mention of prayer which always accompanied fasting in Israel?

As to Esther's ignorance of the impending fate of the Jews, it may well be that the harem environment has protected her from the knowledge. It seems clear that at least the servants know that she is Jewish. They knew that Mordecai is a Jew (chapter 3); they are also aware of Haman's plans; servants know everything anyway. We must assume that they have decided to protect her, both from the knowledge of Haman's plans and from being discovered as a Jew. Therefore, they tell Esther of Mordecai's behavior, for they are afraid that it may attract attention to the relationship between the two. The first goal is to get Mordecai to stop carrying on in public. What is shown here is that the life of the dominated group is full of knowledge of which the ones who are in charge have no notion. Ahasuerus does not know what every servant in the palace knows, that the woman he chose to make his queen is a member of the people who will perish by his consent. Esther is shown living in a kind of false innocence, isolated in her monotonous harem existence; she alone has not heard of the royal proclamation. Perhaps she did not want to know—what can she do anyway? Her beauty is no longer sufficient to give her power, for the king no longer asks for her.

When Mordecai calls on her, facing her with the evidence of what is to happen, her reply to him sounds ironic and bitter. Since all the people know, how is it that Mordecai does not know that going to the king without being invited incurs the gravest risk? One can almost see her shrug her shoulders as she says, "As for me, I have not been invited to enter the king's presence for these thirty days." I have not been invited, and I will not be is the implication.

Mordecai's words are terse and direct and not exactly kind: you won't escape anyway, so why not try and persuade the king? What have you got to lose? Many people think that there is at least an allusion to divine protection in the phrase "escape and deliverance will arise for the Jews from another quarter" (vs. 14). If this is true, the allusion is so hidden as to be insignificant. The upshot of Mordecai's words to Esther is that she has only one chance of survival and that is by going to the king. It may be that her languishing in the royal harem was for a purpose after all. These words serve to convince Esther who calls for a fast in her behalf. There is again the sense of a mental shrug in the words "If I perish, I perish." She would probably rather perish with honor. The chapters to follow will show that she will give her intercession all that she has got.

Esther's character shows a decided change in this episode. She does not simply do what Mordecai commands, as she did earlier (see 2:20). She is in charge; in the end, when she has consented to Mordecai's request, she gives him instructions instead of the other way around. As a matter of fact, Mordecai gives her no precise instructions; he leaves the "how" of the intercession up to her and apparently is confident to do so. Esther is beginning to come into her own as the main mover of events.

The listener knows that she will go to the king and a sense of risk and suspense has been built. Although there seems to be no outside support for the prohibition quoted in vs. 11 the truth of it is undeniable. The king holds the power of life for Esther in his hands.

Esther is in the position of one who is at the mercy of those around her; even the servants know more than she does. Yet she is the one who is called on to save her people. As one of the multitude of women in the harem she has no power, and is like Ruth a most unlikely redeemer. She is willing to bank on the "who knows" of Mordecai. She will not go to the king as the woman who counted on her beauty and charm to win people, she will go in the full knowledge that her chances are slim but they are her only chances. And who knows. . . .

Before she can do anything Esther has to come face to face with reality; she has to discern the situation for what it is: a crisis situation. (Mordecai calls it twice a "time like this"; vs. 14.) Once she discerns the time as such she can move into activity.

In preaching from this passage one could take vs. 14 as the focus. The "you" in the verse is the Esther we have just described. One should be careful not to make an easy identification with Esther since the preacher and the listener are more correctly seen in the role of Haman or the king. There is something starkly secular about this episode. We should probably resist the temptation to see religious implications where there are none. The narrator resisted this temptation. No prayer is mentioned at the most obvious place where prayer would have been most logical, at the mention of the fast.

Yet, we should not forget that it concerns here the life of the faithful, the people of Israel. The life of God's people is at stake, and help will come from unexpected quarters. As with

Ruth, we encounter in Esther a person in a most unlikely position to do anything constructive who prepares herself to change the course of events. Esther personifies the chance of life for her people.

It is telling that she plans to engage in a communal fast. As preparation for her act of civil disobedience on behalf of the community, she draws the community around her as a protective circle. Her words "Then I will go to the king against the law; if I perish, I perish" (vs. 16) have been paraphrased by others who engaged in similar activity after her; we think, for example, of Martin Luther King's last speech in Memphis, Tennessee, and the lines: "I don't know what will happen now. . . . But it doesn't matter with me now, because I've been to the mountain top. And I don't mind." Esther should be placed in the line of people for whom the dream did not become reality but who remained true to their calling to civil disobedience in order to rise with their people.

A Dinner Invitation
(Esther 5:1–8)

Esther remains in the center of the stage in this episode. She stations herself strategically to catch the king's attention and when she does, she wins the first round as the king stretches his scepter to her. So far, so good; she will not instantly die. Moreover, the king, recognizing the petitioner, asks her graciously what she wants. Esther makes her second move by inviting the king and his advisor Haman to dinner. While they are there, the king repeats his inquiry and Esther invites them to come back in response. On the morrow she will tell them what is on her mind.

The units in this section are full of the *m-l-k* sound (from *mlk* meaning "to rule"). The royalty surrounding Esther is emphasized to indicate her lack of power and influence. Her royal robes (vs. 1) are a travesty of power, her title of queen a mere honorific and symbol of her weakness. Her physical position is explained in detail to point to her strategy: she is close, but not too close. We notice the key phrase "she found favor in his eyes" (vs. 2). The introductory unit (vss. 1–2) has the people in their place, there sits the king, there stands Esther . . . we hold our breath . . . and there comes the scepter.

The following units (vss. 3–5, 6–8) are parallel in form.

Each opens with the king asking Esther what she wants and
Esther's reply as the response. Both times the king's questions are almost identical. Twice he asks what she desires,
and each time promises that nothing will be too much ("if
half the kingdom ..." vss. 3 and 6). The double question on
the part of the king has the effect of condescending kindness
toward his forgotten queen. He even calls her by her forgotten title, "Queen Esther." Esther replies formally and with
elaborate courtesy. In her first reply she issues an invitation
to dinner, implying that on this occasion she will reveal what
she is after. At the dinner she is even more elaborately courteous. She begins, "I ask and request ..." (vs. 7), stops in
mid-sentence to interrupt herself with polite phrases, "If I
have found favor in the eyes of the king and if it pleases the
king ...," then issues a second dinner invitation.

While everything is set for action the narration slows to a
standstill in this section. This slowing down is so gradual,
moreover, that in the end we feel we are going nowhere. As
once Ruth, here Esther waits upon the favorable word of the
one who has power over her life. She is patient and knows
how to speak the right word at the appropriate time, much
like the sage who writes that "a word in season is good"
(Prov 15:23), and "a word fitly spoken is like apples of gold in
a setting of silver" (Prov 25:11), or better yet, that "with pa-
tience a ruler may be persuaded, and a soft tongue will break
the bone" (Prov 25:15).

To the king, the first dinner invitation probably comes as
a pleasant surprise. Esther wants nothing more after all than
to entertain the king and his most trusted advisor. He is obviously fond of eating and drinking, as we have learned from
the previous chapters, and can already imagine the delica-
cies which will be set before him. Small wonder that the king
tells Haman to hurry.

Esther knows the effectiveness of a well-planned and executed dinner. Thus, one expects her to make her request at
some time during the party. Yet, once more she puts it off. It
is possible, of course, that she is getting cold feet, but it is
more likely that she is carefully preparing the moment. Unlike the feasting that has gone on before in the story, Esther's
feast moves purposefully toward its desired end. By putting
the request off, she makes a good impression on the king. Her

interest is apparently more in pleasing him than in getting
what she wants. She also piques his curiosity. What on earth
could she want? And, thirdly, the second invitation increases
Haman's self-confidence, which will serve its own ends.

From the point of character development, the king responds much as one would expect. He has an eye for beauty,
and so Esther's presence is noticed. He is generous, so he
promises her half of his kingdom. He has a taste for good
food and drink, so he accepts the invitations with alacrity.
Impetuous and impressionable, he causes one to smile at his
gullibility. Haman will be in the center of the stage in the
next episode and we will wait to describe him.

Esther shows here of what she is capable. She stands
alone in the courtyard, there are no advisors to tell her what
to do and what to say. Her community, though present with
her in the communal act of fasting, cannot help her in this
moment. She fears for her life, and if she loses her life, her
people are lost also. She wisely waits until the king notices
her, she does not push herself into the foreground, and proceeds to play on his weakness. Apart from everything else,
the first dinner gives her time to reconnoiter, to discern the
mood of the king and the power of Haman.

Haman at Home
(Esther 5:9–14)

In the next two episodes (vss. 9–11, 12–14) the focus is on
Haman. He is on his way home, full of himself, feeling on top
of the world, and again faces Mordecai's impudence on the
way out of the palace grounds. Once home, he regales his
family and friends with the story of his success.

In a speech he describes the extraordinary honor he is re-
ceiving from Queen Esther, and how it all means nothing
when he faces Mordecai. His wife and friends know how to
solve that problem. Why wait until the pogrom? Have
Mordecai executed right away! You don't realize your power,
they say. Of course the king will listen! The gallows will be
ready. Come on, it will make you feel so much better! The
chapter ends with Haman's having the instrument of execution erected.

These verses are full of irony. Haman's inflated ego is
even more inflated when he leaves the exalted company of

queen and king. His place in the world is now certainly secure. Around him the people bow, giving witness to his greatness and power. Except the one character, the one who will
"not move on his account," Mordecai. The more the oppressor gains in power and strength, the less will the oppressed
acknowledge this strength. Yet Haman controls his fury. He
rushes home and there gathers his own around him. Basking
in their admiring glances, he begins to toot his own horn.
Here is a group of admirers who will make him forget miser-
able Mordecai. "On top of everything, I am now becoming an
intimate of the queen," he says. "And you know what? It all
means nothing when I see Mordecai, that Jew, who won't
move when he sees me!"

His wife and friends do not quite understand what he is so
bothered about. Surely, here is an easy problem to solve. Get
rid of the Jew, the thorn in his flesh. An extraordinarily high
gallows, or stake, represents the measure of the height to
which Haman has risen. Upon it, the man who will not move
before Haman will squirm. Since he will not bow, he shall
hang. It is simple, after all. Those who will not bow will
break. A good example, too. And Haman has no objection; he
wonders why he did not think of it himself. So he has the tree
of death made, and the shadow of death on the story becomes
more threatening. A part of the story which began with feasting ends in impending destruction.

Chapter 5 is not an easy one to preach from. It is possible
to use it instead as an introduction to a sermon on, for example, chapter seven. If one chooses chapter five as a text for a
sermon, it might be most effective to preach the sermon as
one of a series on this book. Thus, the character of the entire
story can be highlighted, tensions maintained, and developments shown.

In chapter five there are two people who are on the way
toward something. Ostensibly, Esther may be on her way to
death, Haman toward more influence and power. Of the two
people, one aims at the salvation of a people, the other at the
destruction of the same people. The fact that the objective of
the two characters is toward the same people is hidden in the
telling of the story.

The outcome of the story will push the characters in opposite directions from where they *seem* to be going, but that

denouement is yet to come. The possibility of this development is hinted at already. Esther survives the first audience with the king and the odds look to be more in her favor. Haman clearly overreaches himself more and more. A stake seventy-five feet high no less! In circumstances and character these two people are in contrast to each other. One is by social and cultural custom on the low rungs of the ladder of power and prestige. Since she is a woman, she is *par excellence* the one who is manipulable. She is, moreover, alone, living in isolation from the community that could sustain and advise her. Her title of queen is more a joke than an honor; here is truly a queen of no-people. The events around Queen Vashti have shown how easily such royal personages are disposed of.

The other, Haman, has everything going for him. Wealth, influence, power—another "man of substance." He is surrounded by his family and friends who listen to him and advise him. In character they are a study in contrast. Esther is patient, speaks the right words at the right time, positions herself in the right place. Haman is a hot-tempered tyrant who restrains himself with difficulty in the face of Mordecai's impudence. He is a braggart, who has to point out to his environment how well he is doing.

Caught between these two, His Majesty seems to be the most helpless. He, who probably thinks he knows what is going on, is constantly in the dark. Until the last, he is unaware who the people are that he is setting up for destruction, who his queen is, and who Haman is. Some of his ignorance is self-induced, no doubt, as will be played out in the next chapter. The seemingly impotent power for good embodied by Esther, the seemingly unstoppable force of evil embodied by Haman, and in between the seemingly powerful powerless king create a mood of tension and expectancy. And God? Should we see God as hiding in the shadows, directing this play, pulling the strings? The storytellers do not say. The fate of God's people is in weak hands. Perhaps we do best to see the signs of the kingdom in this very weakness. Instruments of destruction only seem powerful. To see power at work our gaze must look elsewhere, to the garden where Esther stands, half in the shadow, half in the light, until she is noticed.

A Sleepless Night
(Esther 6)

Hidden identities and motives abound in this chapter. More and more it becomes clear as to where the main characters of the story are going to end up. In the flow of the events chapter six functions as an interlude, a crucial one which foreshadows Mordecai's rising and Haman's fall. It also brings Mordecai to the king's attention which prepares the way for his eventual elevation to Haman's former place.

The episode is ironic. First, the king cannot sleep—too much good wine perhaps—and he has his servants read to him. The material sounds dull, "the records of what went on every day," but it turns out to be less dull than one would expect. In these records, it is written that two eunuchs conspired against the king and that Mordecai intervened. The king has forgotten the whole business, including what was done to reward Mordecai. The servants who supply crucial information in this part of the story inform the king that this little item was overlooked and then inform the king that Haman is around to advise him. Haman cannot wait to see Mordecai dead and he is hanging around the court to secure a speedy execution. Just the person who can help me, thinks the king. Then follows the conversation between Haman and the king in which the king does not reveal the identity of the man whom he wants to honor, as Haman formerly hid the identity of the people he wanted to destroy (3:8–11). His self-image is so large that Haman cannot imagine the king wanting to honor anyone but himself and he gives the king directions, with the well-known results. Delightful, says the king, do it and do it quick, for Mordecai the Jew.

So Mordecai is elevated not upon the stake but upon a horse of honor and Haman cries out his honor before him. The one who would not bow is now being acknowledged as honored by the one who demanded honor of him. A splendid role reversal which bodes ill in the eyes of all who know Haman. The last paragraph is full of the word *fall*. In addition the events speed up, so that Haman is dragged to the party which he had so eagerly anticipated in indecorous and ominous haste.

The chapter develops in a manner parallel to chapter five.

An introductory scene is followed by the entrance of Haman, then the focus is on Haman and Mordecai and last on Haman at home. The events proceed in a downward spiral instead of the upward one of chapter five. As Esther in the previous chapter, Haman hangs around the court waiting for the king's attention. He, unlike Esther, is out only for himself. His humiliation before Mordecai is a continuation of the theme of his humiliation before this man and sounds a prelude to his fall which is to come. He is interrupted in the middle of his deliberations with family and friends.

A Queen's Feast
(Esther 7)

Without ado, the chapter opens with Esther entertaining the king and his counselor. The speed of the course of events has not slowed down. We are on the second day of the feast in vs. 2. The king repeats his question to Esther for the third time and this time she answers without further hedging, "Let my life be given to me on my asking and my people on my request" (vs. 3). "Let my life be given"—three words in Hebrew which make the urgency of the situation immediately clear. Esther guarantees the king's attention by this manner of presenting the case. The life of her people depends on her life at this point.

In the next verse she repeats the three terms for the holocaust used earlier (3:13): "destroy, slay, and annihilate." They are the terms in the written decree for the destruction of the Jews. If, she says, if it had been merely a matter of being sold into slavery she would not have bothered the king (RSV: "for our affliction is not to be compared with the loss to the king;" more likely read: "for it would not be proper to bother the king with such an injury").

The king, with his selective memory, does not recall the particulars and asks who is responsible. Esther points to Haman, who must have been aware of what was happening by then, "An enemy and adversary, this wicked Haman here!" (vs. 6). The king runs outside and Haman quickly decides to throw himself on the mercy of the queen, "for he saw that evil was determined against him by the king" (vs. 7). He is now on a downhill slide and doomed to make one bad decision after another, for the king, finding him on Esther's couch on his return, draws the wrong conclusion. Apparently no act is low enough for this scoundrel. "Would he even assault the queen in my presence, my own house?" cries the king (vs. 8).

These words are strong enough to seal Haman's fate which is indicated by the fact that they cover his face. Although little is known of the latter action as a regular custom, one understands immediately, even today, that this covering is a symbol of Haman's condemnation.

One of the servants lends a helping hand in delivering the final blow. "Look," says Harbonah, "there is already a gallows." "So they hanged Haman on the gallows which he had erected for Mordecai and the anger of the king abated" (vs. 10). So ends this chapter.

Guideposts

There are four possible subdivisions of this chapter. The first unit presents the king and Haman at Esther's feast and Esther's request (vss. 1–4). The king repeats his earlier question to Esther and this time, the magical third, she does not hesitate to come out with it. The putting of her own life first is both diplomatic and realistic. The effect is to catch the king's attention right away; the life of her people is not worth anything without her intercession. She emphasizes the seriousness of the threat by the three-fold repetition of the words of destruction. By this time Haman must be sitting up and paying attention; even though the king does not realize what and who is involved, Haman certainly does.

The next unit (vss. 5–6) introduces the lifting of the threat for the Jews in a roundabout way. First, the king asks who is responsible for the dastardly plan, which deflects the attention toward Haman. He, the king, is responsible also, but this fact is tactfully not mentioned by Esther, who puts the full blame on Haman. Then Haman begins to quake in earnest, and he is about to make his next and final mistake. The words of the brief interchange between king and queen have an almost rhythmic quality. In typical fashion the king asks a double question, and Esther replies with three descriptive terms for Haman. The king: "Who is he, and where is he?" Esther: "Enemy, adversary, wicked Haman" (vs. 6).

The next unit (vss. 7–8) opens with the anger of the king.

It does not say with whom the king is angry, but he goes for a walk, presumably to cool off. Haman interprets the king's anger as being directed toward him and stays with the queen "ready to beg for his life." This last mistake is also his worst, and will cost him his life. In counting on the tenderness of a woman's heart, he appears to be after her body. If the king still had problems deciding what to do with Haman, who had after all been a servant he once held in high esteem, the scene that meets his eye on the king's return quickly tilts the balance. Whether the king really thought that Haman was ravishing Esther or not, the situation provides him with a ready excuse for proceeding with the execution. The king returned "just as Haman was falling" (vs. 8). The word *fall* which was used with such ominous overtones by his family is here used in connection with Haman for the last time. He has now fallen indeed. And he is literally falling in the pit he dug for someone else when they hang him on the gallows that he had intended for Mordecai.

Once more a servant provides a suggestion which moves the events quickly toward a satisfactory solution in the last unit (vss. 9–10) in the form of Harbonah's advice. The gallows had only been there for a short while but the servants know all about it and for whom it is meant. Mordecai, whose word saved the king, was supposed to hang upon it!—a reminder which recalls for the king exactly who Mordecai is and what he did for the king and how he was honored. Obviously, this is the place for Haman; his hanging where he wanted Mordecai to hang satisfies one's sense of justice. Again a chapter ends with an execution. All is quiet: "Then the anger of the king abated" (vs. 10).

Questions and Suggestions

Not everything is revealed in this episode, not everything is resolved. In the opening scenes the main characters are all hiding something or something is hidden from them. Haman and the king are not aware of Esther's identity or her relationship to Mordecai. The king does not know that Haman had it in for Mordecai and how he has humiliated Haman by making him cry out the good news about Mordecai. Esther, presumably, does not know of the events concerning Mordecai described in the previous chapter, since she makes no use of what would have been such welcome information. All the ingredients for a classical comedy are present.

A question arises as to whether the king is aware, insofar as he remembers anything about it, that the people whose destruction is being prepared are the Jews. One would think that he is not, since he does seem to realize that Mordecai is a Jew. (See 6:10, where the king refers to Mordecai as "Mordecai the Jew.") Surely, had the king known about the impending doom of the Jews, he would have taken some action to exempt Mordecai at least. One does not know for sure with this king, since he does not seem to do a lot of thinking on his own, but the likelihood is that the identity of the particular people is not known to the king when Esther begs for her life and that of her people. The question of the king, "Who is this?" would have sounded more logical if it had gone "Who are these people?" Be that as it may, it remains until a later time for Esther to reveal the identity of her people (8:5). In the meantime it is satisfactory to have described in detail the downfall of Haman whose rise and plotting received much attention in what preceded. A sense of balance is restored and no one feels sorry when they see him on the gallows.

There is an implication that Haman was loved by no one. As his own wife and counselors seem almost indecently quick with their predictions of his fall, so are the means for his final destruction pointed out with what amounts to alacrity by one of the servants. Such power as Haman held, by violence and unjust means, by constantly bringing home his elevated position to those below him, is usually resented, and no one much regrets to see the tyrant go. In the development of the story, the events described here, as well as in the first verses of the following chapter, serve as a deflection from the main purpose which is the saving of the Jews. Only Esther has been saved so far. The comedy of errors which surrounds Haman also serves to relax the tension about the fate of the Jews. At the end of the chapter this tension rises again when the shadow of the gallows once more falls over the story.

A possible sermon focus would be vs. 3, the request of Esther: "Let my life be given to me on my asking and my people on my request." What does it mean to ask for one's life? Who are the people who do such asking, who are the ones with power to give life in the story? In this context the character development in the story should be used to the full. Esther who has only *seeming* power, who is as a woman and a foreigner entirely without outside resources, shows her true mettle in this part of the story. She has been patient; now she speaks quickly and to the point. The importance of a "word spoken at the right time" could be illustrated by both contemporary illustrations and incidents from the Bible.

Those in power to give or take life are much the same today as they were yesterday. The king and Haman are both types of those who wield power. One does it capriciously and by being manipulated, the other, by steadfastly planning the destruction of an entire people, is much more methodical and oriented towards a certain goal.

Esther asks not only for her own life but for that of her people, which puts her request beyond the limits of self-interest. The life of the people is of concern to God who is considered to be the life giver in Israel's tradition. (See, for example, Ps 80 as an illustration of the way in which God is held responsible for the life of the people.) This means, of course, that God is ultimately concerned for the life of the world, to which the incarnation gives witness. Ultimately, it is not Ahasuerus or Esther who saves the people but their life is in God's hands rather than in that of the Purim. Yet, this fact does not take our responsibility towards one another away.

Finally, the God to whom the Bible gives witness was and is especially concerned with the life of Israel. This knowledge makes us as Gentiles especially responsible for the life of the Jews, and we stand therefore especially convicted when this life is threatened and endangered as it was during the years of the Second World War. Such responsibility does not demand from us an uncritical stance toward the state of Israel and its policies, but it does enforce a posture of repentance and advocacy During the Second World War the evil of Haman was let loose upon the world. In the story of Esther, Haman is dead; let us pray that Esther is not "just a story."

Although typological explanations should be handled

with great delicacy and care, in Esther as in Ruth we find
precursors of the Messiah, the sort of people throughout the
Bible who are called and who remind us of the Messiah, even
if they do not make it altogether.

Harvest of Destruction
(Esther 8)

We might well wish that the story had ended with the
previous chapter but it does not. Haman is dead, but the evil
he intended is very much alive. The seeds of destruction that
were sown by him will yet see a harvest, a harvest which is
described in chapters eight and nine. There are several considerations to be raised before we discuss the last units of
Esther. The unhistorical character of this narrative should be
kept in mind. Esther is a Brer Rabbit story, the story of a
people who, languishing under persecution, keep hope and
spirits alive by the tall tale of Esther, the trickster who out-
witted all those in power and thus saved the life of the
victims.

The irony of the story becomes more and more apparent.
Victims become warriors; the fear of them falls on all the
peoples (vs. 16) and many people seek identification with the
Jews, in an ironic reversal of the true situation. Imagine! Instead of the Jews' having to identify themselves as those
marked for destruction, as they were obligated to in the
Hitler years, people flock to their ranks and want to be identified as Jews.

The king, sillier than ever, is pictured as rejoicing in the
destruction of his own subjects to a ludicrous extent. When
he points out the numbers of dead in the city he says, "What
then have they done in the rest of the provinces!" (9:12). As
Jones has pointed out, "Surely, the author did not expect his
readers to keep a straight face while hearing the great king
rejoice that so many of his own subjects have been killed" (in
Moore [ed.], p. 447).

The people killed by the Jews are those who after hearing
about the second edict are foolish enough to attack anyway.
"Who would be so stupid as to observe Haman's obsolete
edict, not knowing of the second one, published more effi-
ciently? The answer is that 800 people in Susa and 75,000 in
the provinces were so stupid" (Jones, in Moore [ed.], p. 446).

On the serious side, these chapters show what hatred and persecution are capable of creating. One of the most dreadful repercussions of oppression is that it may re-create the former victims into a mirror image of the former oppressors. One of the aftermaths of war is often perpetuated hatred. Insofar as the existence of the state of Israel is the result of the Second World War and the Holocaust, it should be remembered what horrifying bloodshed gave birth to a nation. As it should be remembered that the persecutions and pogroms which loom in the background of the Esther tale are terrifyingly real. The other side of the stupidity mentioned above is the cruelty of those who are ready to "destroy, slaughter, and annihilate."

In the meantime, as outsiders, we should not be too quick to frown on the motivation given for Purim, not those of us who celebrate the Fourth of July. One of the difficulties of Esther for the church is that we have no festival that is equivalent to Purim. On the positive side, this fact has prevented the church from usurping a Jewish festival; on the negative side, this fact puts a barrier in the way of identifying with the book for Christians. Yet, if we think of our own national festivals which celebrate deliverance from oppression in the past, we should not find it too difficult to seek identification through analogous experiences.

Perhaps these considerations could be useful for a sermon preached on an occasion such as Independence Day. If a series of sermons is preached on Esther a last sermon on chapters 8 and 9 is necessary to conclude the series in accord with the narrator. One might read from them selectively, since the style is extremely elaborate and tedious in places, in contrast to the preceding chapters. Another possibility for the use of these chapters in preaching is to let them illustrate points made in a sermon on chapter seven.

Guideposts

While in the previous chapter the word Jew is missing, in chapter eight it occurs in every unit. The introduction to the chapter (vss. 1–2) briefly describes the success of Esther which extends to Mordecai. The role reversal, already indicated at the end of chapter six, is now complete: "the king took off his signet ring, which he had taken from Haman, and

gave it to Mordecai. And Esther set Mordecai over the house
of Haman" (vs. 2).

And yet, although Haman is dead, and Esther and
Mordecai are faring well, the fate of the Jews is still hanging in the balance. The next unit (vss. 3–6) has Esther be-
seeching the king on behalf of her people, proving that her
words spoken earlier were not merely centered on herself
and therefore to an extent empty of meaning. When she
asked for her own life, she added the life of her people (7:3),
and here she makes the interest in the life of her people
real. The concern and the interest of this book are in the life
of the people, the community and its survival, rather than
in individuals. Esther broaches the matter in her most elaborately polite style: "If it please the king, if I have found
favor . . .; if the matter seem right and if I am pleasing in
his eyes" (vs. 5). She is aware that the king might be getting
tired of her requests.

Indeed, the king's reply has just a tinge of weariness, a
weariness which serves Esther and Mordecai well since it
leaves not only the execution but also the organization of
their plans up to them, the king giving them *carte blanche*.
The king responds to Esther's request by pointing to what he
has done so far, "the house of Haman I have given to Esther"
(vs. 7), and to what has been done to Haman, "him they
hanged from the gallows." One almost expects a "haven't I
done enough?" Rather, he puts the entire burden of reversing
the edict of Haman on Esther and Mordecai: "Now, you
yourselves write in regard to the Jews" (vs. 8). Then follows
the elaborate description of the royal apparatus, once more
set in motion as it had been before—once to denounce Queen
Vashti (1:21–22), once to organize the destruction of the Jews
(3:12–15). This time the edict is to prepare for the restoration
of the Jews. Vss. 9–15 present an elaborate variation on
3:12–15, with the roles reversed: from passive victims the
Jews are transformed into defenders of their lives according
to the law of the king.

A final unit (vss. 15–17) emphasizes Mordecai's elevation.
He can now truly accept a change of clothes; sack and ashes
are changed into a "royal robe of blue and white" (vs. 15).
Then follows a description of the reaction in Susa and among
the Jews.

A People's Feast
(Esther 9)

This chapter can be divided into two major sections: the first (vss. 1–16) is devoted to the story of the destruction of the enemies of the Jews; the last (vss. 17–32) is concerned with the feast of Purim, how it got established and some of its customs.

These major sections have their own subdivisions. A first unit fixes the time of the events to follow (vss. 1–4). Vss. 5–11 recount the numbers of those killed in Susa. Vss. 12–15 record Esther's final request. Vss. 16–19 tell of the number of people killed in the provinces and begin the account of the institution of Purim. Vss. 20–23 describe the institution of Purim with letters from Mordecai. Vss. 24–25 offer a brief explanation of the festival. Vss. 26–28 record the establishing of Purim and vss. 29–32 state Esther's authority in the matter. Chapter ten provides a postscript of a few verses that refer to the greatness of the king and Mordecai and to further sources for reading about them.

The most disturbing matter in this part of the story is Esther's last request of asking for another day of killing. The most acceptable way out is probably to agree with Moore that in chapter nine especially "demands of law and cult completely outweigh any dramatic consideration," and that "Esther's request is best regarded simply as a literary device by the author to provide a 'historical' basis for the conflicting dates of celebrating Purim" (Moore, p. 90, 91). In addition, we keep in mind that the Bible is not intended to provide us with models to follow. There are no heroes and antiheroes in the Scripture. The Word tells of the way God goes with these people, such people as Esther, as we. Unless one would agree to a wholesale condemnation of the contemporary hunt for Nazis who operated in the concentration camps we should be careful in condemning Esther's request which is all too human.

Suggestions

Vss. 24–25 contain the one reflective section of this chapter which provides us with at least the possibility for a sermon. In them is described the past history—Haman and his evil plans, the intercession of Esther, and how Haman's plans came to naught. The content is not precisely in agreement with all that has gone on in the tale but it sums up the salient facts: Haman, the enemy of the Jews, planned a pogrom and to determine the day had Pur, that is, the lot, cast. Then Esther came before the king. What follows in Hebrew reads literally, "Then she came before the king and he said in a letter." Most translations, correctly interpreting that Esther is meant by "she," read, "Esther came before the king." By doing this we may on the other hand lose an emphasis and contrast which the Hebrew has kept. When *she* came. Who is *she*? She is the woman, the Jewess, Esther. With the word *she*, the lack of power and status is brought out that would of necessity accompany this identification. In contrast to *she* stands the "he" of the king, who says and it comes to pass. The sentence has Esther and the king taking care of the whole matter. It may be that succinctness was the cause of any contradictions with what is told in chapters 3–7.

One word which occurs three times in these two verses is the word for "plans," in either the noun or the verbal form (RSV "plot" and "devised"). It may be helpful if we consider this word together with the word Pur. Haman plotted to do evil to the Jews and he cast the Pur to that end. His plans are changed. The Hebrew uses the word for "to turn around" (*shuv*) in a key place. It is the king who changes the plans but the terms are too loaded not to reveal the providence of God at work. The same change of plans is mentioned in Gen 50:20 in regard to Joseph, where Joseph says to his brothers, "As for you, you planned evil against me but God planned it for good." The same word is used for "plan" in both texts. The sense of the text is not that God would be the "jack-in-the-box" who comes up with the unexpected appearance, but that God's providence is working itself out through human love and concern. It was Esther who counterplanned the evil of Haman. And so the feast is called "Purim," the feast of "chance." And yet it was not chance that saved the people.

Once more laughter runs through this book written for and by a people clinging to hope against all odds, hanging on to faith, hanging on to belief in the love of God. Chance was and is against them but all the plans of chance were brought to naught.

JONAH

Introduction

In Jonah there is no lack of theological issues. In fact there are such a number of them that little agreement exists as to what could be the main concern of this small book. Jonah is a more popular source for preaching than Ruth and Esther. Everyone knows the story, everyone can draw a lesson from it. Jonah is everyone. This overexposure can result in overly simplistic and at times incorrect perceptions about the book. It is easy to condemn Jonah as narrow-minded, a bigoted Israelite quickly to be dismissed by those who know better than to strike such an attitude. We shall see whether narrow-mindedness is indeed Jonah's failing. The book is well constructed, the story told in the classical style of Hebrew narrative.

Date

Most scholars agree that the book is of post-exilic origin but there is a rather wide divergence of opinion on the date that should be assigned within that time span. One notable exception to the unanimity of post-exilic dating is George M. Landes, who does not rule out a time shortly before the fall of Jerusalem in 587 B.C. as a possible date of composition. At the other end of the spectrum we find H. W. Wolff who assigns the work to the third century and certainly will not entertain a date earlier than the fourth. The intricacies of the debate center for a great deal on linguistic considerations. My own inclinations are to put the story closer to the exile, but the safest solution

seems to allow for the wide margin of sixth to third
century B.C.

Literary Category and Structure

In spite of its canonical place among the prophets there is
little similarity between Jonah and the other prophetic
books. There are no visions, no messages, in Jonah; only the
short speech in chapter three records a prophetic saying. The
main part of the book is a story about a prophet and is closer
to the Elijah and Elisha material in the book of Kings than to
other prophetic books. It can be maintained that the book
does not present itself as history. There is not much serious
debate on this score and most everyone agrees that Jonah is
fiction. The question remains as to what kind of fiction this
book represents.

Biblical scholars, not always known for closely defining
their use of literary terms, have labeled it variously "a leg-
end, a fable, a myth, an allegory, a parable," to name a few.
Of these categories that of parable seems to be the best fit-
ting. A parable is a story which teaches an essential truth
and demands from the listener a judgment. While we know
the parable mostly as a favorite teaching device of Jesus, we
do have a few examples available to us in the OT.

In Hebrew the meaning of the word *parable* sometimes
comes close to that of riddle (Ezek 17:2; 24:3). In addition to
their plainness parables have a hidden quality. All is not as
clear in them as it might seem at first. As Crossan has
pointed out parables "are stories which shatter the deep
structure of our accepted world" (p.122). We should therefore
be on our guard when we are faced with a parable.

Another element which we already mentioned is that of
judgment. The listener is asked to make a decision on the
basis of the parable, a judgment for or against the truth it
teaches. The discomforting part is that often the judgment
we make turns out to be a judgment against ourselves. A
good example of this quality of the parable is the confronta-
tion between Nathan and King David, as recorded in 2 Sam
12. King David thinks that he is pronouncing judgment on
some scoundrel and instead he himself proves to be the one
who is under judgment (2 Sam 12:1–8).

The style of the book of Jonah is satirical, making use of

irony. There are also mythological motifs present, as that of the fish that swallows a human being to spit it up at a later time, as well as motifs from the world of the fable which draws heavily on plant and animal life.

There are many examples of the ironical or satirical style of the book. Let it suffice here to point to Jonah's name. Jonah is identified as the son of Amittai, a name related to the noun for truth and faithfulness. Jonah, the son of faithfulness, "abandons his faithfulness at the first opportunity and speaks truth only under duress, even then not understanding it" (Good, p. 42).

The structure of the book is clear. There are two major episodes. The first one is Jonah at sea as a response to God's call and consists of chapters one and two. The second episode describes Jonah in Nineveh (chapters three and four). Each episode presents a complete story. Chapters three and four serve to uncover motivations and clarify the main point of the story. They give the narrative its theological depth. Chapters one and three each describe Jonah's call and response, but in contrasting fashion, with chapter one presenting a negative, chapter three a positive response. Chapters two and four each record a conversation between Jonah and God. In chapter two this conversation is one-way, a prayer from Jonah to God; in chapter four there is a response from God.

Parallel imagery used in the book consists, for example, of divine intervention by means of animals, the big fish and the worm or by means of natural elements, the big wind in chapter one and the sultry wind in chapter four. On two occasions non-Israelites are the ones at prayer—the sailors on the boat in chapter one and the Ninevites in chapter three. Both groups use the same type of expression for their hope: "Perhaps ..." and "Who knows. ..." The poem in chapter two may not be a part of the original story but we will use it to illustrate the possible setting of such a prayer.

Theology

We said that a parable is a story that teaches an essential truth. While there are other concerns that arise out of the central message, there is one overriding idea which guides the story. In Jonah the central theme is most clearly articulated in 4:2, 11. The full articulation of this theme is anticipated in 1:6 and 3:9, 10 which contain references to the mercy of God. In 4:2, Jonah cries to God in reproach, "You are a merciful God and compassionate, slow to anger and abounding in steadfast love and repenting of evil." In the last sentence of the book we find God's final reply to Jonah in the form of a question: "Should I then not have pity?" (4:11).

The overriding concern in Jonah then is with the mercy of God, particularly as this mercy goes out to those who are hostile to Israel. Thus the problem in Jonah becomes one of God's justice. The elect people of God, Israel, are not experiencing the mercy of God to the degree that Nineveh has experienced it. Whether written in the sixth or in the third century, the time for the setting of the story is one in which the promises of God to Israel are being called into question. Faced with the tenuousness of Israel's very existence, Jonah is understandably reluctant to rejoice over the redemption of Nineveh.

As a natural consequence of this concern the book also speaks to the nature and understanding of prophecy in Israel. Jonah goes to Nineveh with a simple message of doom: "Yet forty days and Nineveh will be overthrown" (3:4). This message causes the Ninevites to repent. Far from being announcements of immutable divine decrees, all prophecies have repentance as their goal. As Buber has pointed out, "The true prophet does not announce an immutable decree. He speaks into the power of decision lying in the moment, and in such a way that the message of disaster just touches this power" (Martin Buber, *The Prophetic Faith*, p. 103).

Another concern in Jonah is the relationship between Israel and its neighbors. Jonah is asked to accept the fact that faith may exist among nonbelievers. Their turning to God is as acceptable as Israel's turning. Witnesses to this fact are the responses of God to the sailors in chapter one and to the repenting Ninevites in chapter three. As a matter of fact, these nonbelievers hold up a mirror of piety and faith to the believer Jonah. The pagans are setting an example of faithfulness to the "son of faithfulness."

Not only are the concerns here mentioned applicable to ancient Israel but they are eminently applicable to today. Jonah is well suited for preaching. We should exercise caution when preaching from this book, however, not to take the content at face value. When we begin to uncover the story we may find ourselves in Jonah's place.

One could preach on the whole book with chapter four as a focal point, or take each chapter as a sermon text.

Jonah at Sea
(Jonah 1:1–16)

The first chapter is very briefly described as follows: The prophet Jonah is commanded to go to Nineveh but runs in the opposite direction. Tarshish is probably located in Spain. All goes well until the ship is at sea and a big storm threatens to shipwreck the boat. Jonah is found out as the responsible party by the casting of lots and he offers himself up for sacrifice. The sailors try in vain to ride out the storm and then comply with his request to throw him overboard. The storm ceases and the sailors worship the God of Israel.

Guideposts

The chapter can easily be divided into four sub-units. The opening verses (1–3) introduce the main characters, Jonah and God, and with typical economy of words and speed of action set the scene for the rest of the chapter. God speaks in three imperatives to Jonah: "Arise . . . , go . . . , cry." All three verbs are intended to set Jonah in motion. Indeed Jonah gets up, "so Jonah got up," but not to comply with the Lord's command but "to run to Tarshish," i.e., in the opposite direction from Nineveh. Jonah's haste is indicated by a run of verbs in vs. 3: "Jonah rose to flee. . . ." He went down . . . , found . . . ; he paid . . . went on board to go. . . ."

A key expression in this section are words connected with God's presence, used three times. The evil of Nineveh which has "come up before me" in the Hebrew reads "has come up to my face." Twice it is stated that Jonah flees from the "presence of the Lord" (vs. 3); in Hebrew the expression is "away from the face of the Lord." A last word to mention is *great*, which is one of the most often repeated words in the book.

In typical Hebrew style, stringing sentences and phrases together by the conjunction "and" without qualifiers, the story continues with "And the Lord hurled a great wind . . .," describing the first scene with the sailors trying frantically to

save the ship and Jonah fast asleep in the hull. The tempo
slows down, especially at the point where the captain speaks
to Jonah. God "hurls" and there is "hurling" in response and
more to come. The sailors "hurl" the vessels overboard in an
attempt to lighten the load (vs. 5) and they will later hurl
Jonah overboard (vs. 15) on his request (vs. 12). Jonah who
had been commanded to "arise" has instead "gone down" to
Joppa and once more goes down, this time into the hull, and
falls asleep. All opposite of what God intended him to do. The
word for "sleep" is not that of ordinary sleep but more of
trance and is used for example, of the dreamsleep of the
human being when God is fashioning the woman (Gen 2:12)
and of Abraham when God makes the covenant with him
(Gen 15:21). The captain finds him in his dreamsleep and
commands Jonah to "arise," the human voice repeating the
divine one. The word for "cry" used in the first verses for
crying against Nineveh, i.e., prophesying, is here used of
praying, as it is often. The sailors each cry to their god and
Jonah is advised to do the same. The word translated "call"
or "cry" is a key word for the entire book. A word which will
recur with some frequency in the chapter is that of "fear."
Here it is used in a basic sense of being afraid for one's physical well-being.

A last word to emphasize is *perish*. Much of the concern in
Jonah revolves around life and death. "The issue at stake for
Jonah is thus the question of life and death. God and he disa-
gree as to who should live, and who should die" (Fretheim, p.
49).

Immediately the scene moves to the decision of the sailors
to find the responsible party by the casting of lots and to the
ensuing conversation when the lot falls on Jonah (vss. 7–12).
The conversation is punctuated by questions: "Why . . . what
. . . where . . . what people" culminating in "what have you
done!" (vs. 10). Twice the word *fear* occurs, with different
nuances. Jonah confesses that he "fears the Lord, the God of
heaven" (vs. 9), which is as much as to say which God he
worships. The sailors respond with great fear—literally,
"And the men feared a great fear" (vs. 10; RSV "Then the men
were exceedingly afraid"). Here fear indicates awe rather
than fear for physical survival although some of that more
ordinary anxiety is implied.

The word *evil* occurs twice in the sense of the disaster aris-
ing from the storm. In the first unit it was used of Nineveh
and meant sinful behavior. We find in this unit also the word
great and the verb *to hurl* (vs. 12). Jonah advises the sailors to
"take him up and hurl him."

In Vss. 13–16, the first sentence expresses the hesitation of
the sailors to comply with Jonah's advice. "They tried hard
... but they could not" (vs. 13). Before they actually throw
him in the sea they "cried to the Lord." We find an unexpected group of people praying to the God of Israel. They
pray in lament-form for their life—the invocation ("We beseech thee, O Lord") followed by the petition ("Let us not
perish ... lay not on us") and an expression of confidence
("for thou, O Lord, has done as it pleased thee"). After the
prayer they "hurl" Jonah into the sea and this hurling is successful for the storm ceases. Then, in the concluding verse,
"the men feared the Lord exceedingly" (vs. 16) in an almost
exact repetition of vs. 10, literally, "the men feared a great
fear the Lord." The first conversion of the book is recounted
and the word *fear* has found its resolution.

The narrator skillfully weaves together tradition and surprise. The opening words of the book could introduce any
traditional prophecy: "The word of the Lord came...." The
command that follows sounds as those that came to the
prophet Elijah: "Arise and go" (see 1 Kings 17:8; 18:1; 21:17).
Then everything changes and nothing is as expected when
Jonah is on the run. Certainly not like Elijah.

We have already alluded to the possible irony of Jonah
the "son of faithfulness" behaving in a faithless manner. On
the other hand, the name "Jonah" ("Dove") complies well
with its symbolism which is often that of weakness (Hos
7:11; 11:11; Ps 74:19). The three imperatives issued by God
are met by Jonah's efforts to get away from God, "away from
the presence of the Lord."

In the opening section the narrator, then, makes use of
a conventional prophetic introduction, with a charge rem-
iniscent of the great prophets of the past, which offsets the
response of this prophet as entirely unconventional. There
is, of course, the tradition of the protesting participant, as
Jeremiah or Moses, the difference here being that Jonah
does not speak in protest. He simply does the opposite of

what God wants him to do without any reasons
mentioned.

Immediately God intervenes in the events by causing a
storm on the sea. Ironically, Jonah, on his way from the presence of God, flees to the most feared of all the elements in
Israel's lore, the sea. Jonah is apparently more afraid of God
than of the threatening chaos which the sea represents. So
we find him "fast asleep." Everyone else is involved in trying
to save the ship and themselves but Jonah snores in the hull,
symbolizing his withdrawl from involvement, and in his
dreamsleep anticipates his threatening death. He, who
should have been the one to pray, has to be instructed to do
so by the heathen captain.

As is common to the mind of these people, there must be
someone who is directly responsible for the storm and so the
lots are cast and Jonah is found out. At this point, the tempo
of the story slows to a standstill, as the sailors sit down to ask
Jonah about his background and circumstances, while the
storm rages on around them. Of all the episodes in this chapter, perhaps the most incongruous one is this incident of the
small talk in the midst of the tumult. Jonah provides the
proper answer, which contains another incongruity. He was
on his way to flee from God, who, as he confesses, "created
the sea." He should have known his own tradition better, a
tradition which has the Psalmist proclaim, "Where shall I go
from your Spirit/and where from your presence shall I flee./If
I ascend to heaven you are there;/if I make my bed in hell,
there you are;/if I take the wings of the dawn/and set up my
tent at the farthest sea,/even there your hand shall guide me"
(Ps 139:8–10).

Apparently now Jonah recognizes his foolishness and the
futility of his desires and is ready to say good-bye to the
world, as he will again in the last scenes of the book. He is
quick to be ready to die. Yet, to give him his due, he is here
also shown as willing to not have anyone else go with him,
and he surely speaks out of a generous impulse: "Pick me
up and throw me into the sea, then the sea will quiet down
for you" (vs. 12). In the last episode we find the sailors who
owed Jonah nothing but trouble trying to save him and
themselves, but when nothing works they "hurl" him in
and again they pray, this time to the God of Israel. As yet,

we have not heard a word of prayer from Jonah, the professional. God responds positively to the prayer of the sailors, an indication of things to come when the Ninevites will pray.

Speech in these episodes is telling for the development of both story and characters. God commands Jonah concerning Nineveh, "that great city," to "cry" concerning its "evil." The message is left vague, as it will be later on; it is only from Jonah's words that we have an idea of what was intended (see 3:4). Jonah, who is trying to do the impossible, getting away from God, is everywhere met by questions. This questioning becomes especially forceful at the incongruent small talk aboard ship during the tempest. Jonah's answer is noteworthy. He identifies himself indeed as to his antecedents, but the remainder of his answer does not fit the questions. Or does it? He is a Hebrew who fears the Lord, the God of heaven. Perhaps we may imagine a grim smile as he gives his answer. I fear the Lord, that is to say, I am a professional Godfearer! And look where it got me! The sailors continue in their questioning voice and Jonah's reply comes stark and uncompromising: pick me up and hurl me into the sea. All of Jonah's actions so far are questionable. What on earth does he think he is doing, trying to get away from God and away from his occupation, his God-given task? A beginning of an answer is glimmering in Jonah's willingness to make his final descent into the sea. Jonah is not willing to compromise. He suspects already what the result of his prophecy in Nineveh will be. Unless we mistrust his later outburst recorded in chapter four, he had a good idea that God would be merciful to Nineveh. In view of Israel's suffering this means that "God has the unjust continuing to live and the just experiencing death. If this is the way things are to be, then life is absurd. Death is much to be preferred to life with a God such as this" (Fretheim, p. 49).

The last speech recorded in the chapter is the prayer of the sailors. By putting their prayer in the accepted, recognizable form of the lament, the storyteller indicates a major theme of the book: the willingness of unexpected groups of people to turn to God and the acceptability of this conversion. Already the wideness of God's mercy is apparent, when the sailors' prayer is accepted and answered.

Questions and Suggestions

It is unclear as to what Jonah is to announce in Nineveh. Neither is it clear why he flees. He himself will later provide a reason, but at this point it is left to the imagination. The city chosen for the prophecy, called "that great city," is truly appalling. Swollen with violence, it is described by Nahum as "the bloody city/full of lies and booty . . ./hosts of slain/heaps of corpses,/dead bodies without end" (Nahum 3:1,3). It could then be supposed that Jonah flees out of fear. Yet, in what follows he is not revealed as someone who is afraid. He goes to the sea which represented danger and chaos to the Israelite; he sleeps during the raging storm and without hesitation offers himself for sacrifice. It is more likely that Jonah is unwilling to compromise. He will not compromise himself by bringing God's word to the nest of corruption that is Nineveh and so cooperate in the absurdity of God's mercy.

The question where the presence of God is to be found could well be the focus for a sermon. The presence of the Lord is a central theme for the chapter. People who should know better flee the presence and an unexpected crowd is found in the presence. The presence of God in the story is basically a saving presence; the destructive tools, the storm and later the worm, are precisely that, tools to educate Jonah.

There existed in Israel a tension between the desire to localize the presence of God and the knowledge that God's presence cannot be found in a place. Every faith localizes the presence of the Deity to an extent. Judaism and Christianity are no exception to this fact. For Israel, the presence was located in a special way in the temple, and the ark; for Christianity the presence of God is located in a special way in the Word preached and broken. At the same time Israel maintained that the presence of God was too free and too great to be limited to a place and a time. Psalm 139, quoted earlier, witnesses to this belief. The free presence of God is especially represented by God's Spirit. In Hebrew the word for spirit and wind is the same. It is telling that the first sign of God's presence in the story after Jonah's flight is that of the "mighty wind" ("spirit") on the sea.

Jonah fights the merciful presence of God because it makes a mockery of all human ideas of the justice of God. He knows that he cannot escape the presence of God and yet he tries to the utmost. For surely he does not expect to survive being hurled into the sea. He, who should have *gone up* to cry to Nineveh, now *goes down* indeed into the uttermost depths.

Our task, as preachers, is to set up a sense of identification with Jonah, so we can recognize ourselves in him. It should be fairly easy to find contemporary analogies for Nineveh. Jonah is asked to go there to preach God's message and he will not take the message to the enemies of his people and his God. The quotation from Nahum is helpful to articulate the violent image of Nineveh.

Jonah, as a parable that teaches about the mercy of God, teaches also about the human response to that mercy. Jonah shows how staunchly we hold on to our notions of what God should be like. The notion that we are not in charge of how the mercy of God is apportioned may be one of the most difficult ones to change. The club mentality which reigned in Israel is equally strong in the church. We know who are in and who are out.

In the meantime, in the Jonah story, it is finally time for Jonah to pray.

The Prayer of Jonah
(Jonah 1:17—2:10)

As God's intervention is absent in Esther, so it is present in Jonah. Every chapter either begins with an activity on God's part or consists for a great deal of divine interference with the natural state of affairs. In episode two, God first "appoints" a fish, then speaks to the fish. First, the fish swallows Jonah, then it obediently spits Jonah out. Jonah has finally reached the point where he can pray and this episode consists for the most part of his prayer. The belly of the fish is symbolic of the depths to which Jonah has gone in order to avoid God. This animal which is appointed by God at the same time symbolizes God's presence for Jonah, who is saved by means of the fish. Undoubtedly, there is an intended irony here. The one who sought to escape by boat ends up in a fish, ordered for the purpose by the Almighty. A dumb animal becomes in the end the means of Jonah's deliverance.

Guideposts

The episode should probably begin with the last verse of chapter one: "And the Lord appointed a great fish to swallow up Jonah; and Jonah was in the belly of the fish three days and three nights. And Jonah prayed to the Lord, his God, from the belly of the fish, saying . . ." (1:17—2:1). These lines, together with the concluding line of chapter two, form the prose frame for the prayer which is in the form of a traditional poem, a psalm of lament.

We need not spend our time discussing the possibility of being swallowed whole by a fish and living to tell the tale. The storyteller obviously means the fish to symbolize Jonah's experience of the absence of God, a sort of dark night of the soul. The time spent in the midst of the fish—of course it is a "great" fish—is the symbolic three days and nights. At the end of the experience, Jonah is where he began, on dry land.

The prayer is a kind of composite psalm made up of well-known lines from the Psalter. Almost every verse makes up a unit, with the exception of vss. 5 and 6 which can be combined, as can vss. 8 and 9.

The Condition of Prayer

We have said that Jonah is finally ready to pray. He is in the right condition for prayer is what we could have said. It is not to be wondered at that he reaches in his extreme anguish for the beloved lines of those who prayed to their God in need.

Generally speaking, in the Bible the condition of prayer, the posture out of which prayer arises, is that of humanity's state of alienation from God which necessitates the active seeking of God's presence in prayer. It is not by accident that the expression "to call on the name of the Lord" occurs for the first time in the story of the brother murder of Abel by Cain. Prayer is a bridge set up across the breach between God and creation. It is a mark of the complete identification of the Christ with human nature that Jesus prayed, according to the Gospel.

The most common verb used for "to pray" in the OT, and the one used in Jonah 2, has as its root meaning to "intervene, interpose, or mediate." At its core, prayer is the intervention between a world bent on self-destruction and a God who is turned toward this world in love. To seek actively the presence of this God, to call on God's name, involves a turning toward God and with God to the creation.

The two basic categories of prayer are the cry for help and the song of praise. The verb "to cry" or "call" is another verb used for praying as it was in Jonah 1:5,6, and 14. When we read the words "to call on God, or on God's name," we should always hear the echo of "to cry," for this phrase points to the cry for the presence, which arises out of a condition of deprivation and danger, of desperation and urgency.

The cry for help as it is represented in the psalms of lament is born of life "at the edge, where one is sensitive to the raw hurts, the primitive passions," as Brueggemann suggests. The primary experience out of which the lament grows is that of disorder and disorientation (see Walter Brueggemann, *Praying The Psalms*, chapter 1). The psalm is aimed at establishing a reorientation, to use Brueggemann's term, or new order.

The same psalm can evoke the experience of disorientation and reorientation. Most laments contain an "expression of confidence." This expression is not an artificial, tacked-on, forced statement of piety in the midst of distress. Rather, the expression of confidence belongs integrally to the lament and there are only a few psalms of lament which lack it.

The language used for the cry for help is direct in its expressions of grief and pain. There is a gracious allowance made in these prayers for the human heart to pour out all its grief and longing, its sense of alienation, even its desire for vindication, before a God who does not despise the affliction of the afflicted.

The psalm of Jonah describes the condition of disorientation but with a mood of confidence. The entire poem is put in the past tense so one gets the sense that Jonah speaks out of a state of deliverance. Does this mean that the "fish" is experienced as friendly? Far from it. It is important that we recognize the descent of Jonah into the fish as his ultimate descent into chaos. For it is there, precisely there, and in no other place, that he experiences salvation. When he gets his wish and is finally "away from the presence of the Lord," Jonah knows both his deprivation and God's deliverance.

The fish is a monster, just as Nineveh is a monster. In the one as in the other, salvation occurs at the very heart of chaos.

It is possible that as believers and preachers we do not dare dwell enough on the darkness through which the spirit sometimes must go. We tend to slide over "disorientation" rather quickly to the "all is well" state without allowing the experience of darkness to find its full articulation. Far from giving comfort this posture can create a mood of helpless despair in the believer who needs to know at least that one's suffering is participated in by others. The laments offer a great opportunity to articulate the image of the soul in pain. In whichever way the pain is described, at its heart the pain always revolves around the absence of God.

The prayer of Jonah is necessary at this point to provide what has been called a "musical pause." "The prayer of Jonah, that is, the sense-giving, creative, celebrative 'name' by which the prophet speaks of his experience and by which he transfigures chaos into meaning is uttered *in* the fish's belly, not *after* Jonah finds the security of dry land" (Lacocque, pp. 52–53). Whoever put the prayer in this place in the story, whether the original author, or a later redactor, did so wisely.

Guideposts

Psalms of lament usually follow loosely this structure: (1) Address (calling on the name of the Lord); (2) Description of the trouble; (3) Petition (hear me, answer me, etc.); and (4) Expression of confidence/promise of praise. These elements do not always all occur and they may not occur in the same order. Psalm 13 is a good example of a lament with most of the elements represented. Jonah's psalm begins with a reminiscence of crying and being heard; in other words vs. 2 presents a combination of elements 3 and 4. Twice the speaker mentions the cry of distress, "I called, I cried," and twice the cry is balanced by God's answer, "He answered, you heard."

The remembrance of mercy is frequently used in the prayers of Israel, both individual and communal, and reminds us of the crucial place of the remembrance of God's grace for the life of faith. On this reassuring note the next line follows almost strangely: "for you cast me into the deep." This and the following line begin the description of distress. The image of water as representing threat and chaos, here repeated in a fourfold variation, is commonly used in the psalms. Vs. 4 gives the response of the poet to the trouble: "Then I said. . . ." In moving away from God, Jonah found himself outside the presence of God and here recognizes the extent of his deprivation.

Vs. 5 returns to a description of the distress with Jonah describing his "descent" into the "deep." The a/o/u sounds of the original text intensify the ominous quality of the description. The last line of vs. 6 marks the turning point of the experience when the poet exclaims, "And you brought up my life from the pit, Lord my God." The pit is a frequent metaphor in the psalms indicating lack of life, the place of despair. It is often parallel to Sheol; the pit is the image of God's absence.

Vs. 7 disturbs those who see Jonah at the same time abiding in the fish and at the temple of Jerusalem. We should probably not be so literal in our understanding of both the fish and Jonah's prayer. The temple is the symbol for God's presence, the anti-symbol for the pit. "Temple" in the poem's parallelism balances "Lord" and "thee." These lines show the following progression: first the focus is on the self ("my soul fainted within me") and then turns to God ("the Lord, . . . thee . . . thy holy temple").

The prayer ends with a vow, after a reference to idol worship. Both lines can be found elsewhere, but probably only here do they take on an ironic tinge. Here is Jonah, who owes God "true loyalty" and who fled from God, who ended up in the belly of a fish, who boasts of paying vows. There are the pagan sailors, who "pay regard to vain idols," whose prayer God has heard. The wrong people are having God's ear. Yet the prayer ends on a true note: "Deliverance belongs to the Lord!" which sounds almost like a prophecy in light of what is to follow, although Jonah will not be so eager to sing the song of praise on account of others. " 'Deliverance belongs to the Lord!' stands in brilliant incongruity to the limitation which Jonah places on that very deliverance when it comes to the Ninevites" (Fretheim, p. 103).

Fretheim suggests that this line could well be seen as the center of the whole book. "The idea of deliverance, of God's not extending to people what they deserve, is at the very center of the argument between God and Jonah" (p. 104). Certainly, the line could be made the center of a sermon on this chapter. It is the background against which we can view this prayer in its mixture of thanksgiving and distress.

Jonah is not afraid to hold God responsible for what is happening to him: "*You* cast me ... *your* waves and billows ... *you* brought me up." God is held responsible for the life of the person and can be charged when there is lack of life. We notice in the meantime that Jonah does not utter any confession of sin, an element which is often present in a psalm of this kind. Throughout, Jonah is not the one who repents. Even the heathen sailors come closer to a plea for forgiveness than Jonah's prayer. Yet he did find his prayer voice. He recognizes the vital importance of God's presence, and the last line of his prayer stands like a bugle call over the next chapter.

Who Knows
(Jonah 3)

In the most densely constructed chapter of the book, the pivotal action of Jonah's prophecy and its results takes place. When God's word comes to Jonah for the second time he knows better than to try and escape and obediently goes to do his job. The message he is to tell Nineveh is again not articulated. In the next lines we find Jonah striding up and down the streets of Nineveh, "that great city," crying his doomcall: "Yet forty days and Nineveh will be overthrown." The results are first described generally in the reaction of the people and then specifically in the reaction and proclamation of the king. The episode ends with God's decision not to destroy the city on the basis of the conversion of the Ninevites.

Guideposts

The chapter contains two main episodes with an introduction and a conclusion. In the introduction, vss. 1–2, the word of God comes to Jonah again. The wording is almost identical to verse two of chapter one: "Arise, go to Nineveh, that great city, and cry" (RSV "proclaim"). There is a little twist in the sequel which here reads literally "the cry which I myself will speak to you" (RSV "the message that I tell you"). Words for crying are used six times in these ten lines, every time with the root q-r-' with one exception. Just in case Jonah would not know what to cry, God will personally instruct him. The content of the message is probably left deliberately vague, in order to keep the tension in the story from slackening. Nineveh is again called "the great city." This time the phrasing anticipates vs. 3 where the size of the city is described in an extravagant way.

In this chapter, the command of God is followed by the obedient "And Jonah arose," to introduce the first episode (vss. 3–5). Before we hear Jonah's message, it is emphasized how huge the city really was. The size of the city, as the words "that great city," should be understood symbolically for the size of its evil. As the Lacocques point out, "It is an exceedingly great city of three days journey." And not only is it an insurmountable obstacle before Jonah, but its magnitude is commensurate only with its deceptiveness—Nineveh is thus a microcosm of all the falsehood, the crime, the conformism, the solipsism, and the uniform anonymity of the human race. She deserves to be utterly destroyed within forty days because of her "evil way and the violence in their hands" (p. 66). Jonah's message is brief and to the point and reminds the listener of the fate of Sodom and Gomorrah by using the same root for the destruction of Nineveh as was used for that of these two cities (Gen 19:21). There is nothing to suggest that Jonah in his message did not exactly repeat what God told him. No reasons for the impending doom are given, no chance is offered for repentance. An exact and very short time limit is put on the remainder of the city's days. The narrator deliberately presents this message in all its starkness, to bring out a key point of Israelite prophecy. Announced judgment is intended to bring people to repentance.

The Ninevites' response is cast in the traditional language of faith (Gen 15:6; Exod 14:3). The message of Jonah offers no chance for repentance, yet the people are responding in a positive way to God. They "cry out" (RSV "proclaim") a fast and dress in the appropriate garb for mourning and fasting. The next episode (vss. 6–9) is slower in tempo with a focus on the actions and words of a single individual, the king of Nineveh. The king, as the symbol of authority and power, completes the picture of an entire city in mourning. He divests himself of his power by leaving his throne and sitting in sack and ash, as Mordecai at Kingsgate. He also issues a proclamation, literally, "he had it cried around" with a root which primarily means "to cry for help." This root is used, for example, for the Israelites' cry for help to God when they are oppressed in Egypt, and in Jonah for the sailors' cry to their gods in the storm (1:5). Jonah and the king both cry in Nineveh. The king's cry is to repentance and fasting, this time including the animals, and most importantly, the proclamation urges everyone to "cry loudly to God, let everyone turn from their evil ways and the violence that is in their hands" (vs. 8). Then comes the crucial line of the chapter: "Who knows . . . God may turn and repent, and if God turns from his fierce anger we will not perish" (vs. 9). "Who knows. . . ." With this sentence the Ninevite king lets in the possibility of grace. The "perhaps" of the heathen captain of the ship (1:6) sounds once again in the book. Three times in a few lines the word *turn* is used. The Ninevites *turn* from their evil ways, God might *turn* and having turned will not let the people die. To turn in a theological sense always has the connotation of conversion in the Bible. Here the echoes of conversion are present in the most striking way when the word refers to God. The Ninevites are turning to God and they pray that God may turn to them. God does exactly what the Ninevite king had hoped: "When God saw their deeds that they turned from their evil ways, God repented from the evil which God spoke to do them and did not do it." God "repents, is sorry, is consoled," as the root meaning of the verb will have it.

The Ninevites do what God hopes they will do, so God can do what is according to God's nature. The hopes of the people and of God coincide.

Suggestions

The story, true to itself, conjures up the fantastic picture of animals dressed in sackcloth and crying out to God, who "turns" and responds positively to these activities. Unlike the fasting in Esther, here the fast is accompanied explicitly by a loud cry to God. They are a dead people, unless . . . , who knows. . . . The Ninevites fast, like Israel would fast, banking on the goodness and love of God. Some of the language in this chapter is close to that of passages in Jeremiah. Jer. 18:8 spells out the possibility of God's repentance (see also Joel 2:12–14): "if that nation concerning which I have spoken, turns from its evil, I will repent of the evil that I intended to do it." Jonah does not represent an isolated incident of God's "repentance." Nor does it stand alone in its claim of God's care for others than Israel, even Israel's enemies. Amos, in a much earlier age, already announced this theme (Amos 9:7).

The possibility of "outsiders" being the beneficiaries of God's grace, especially if these "outsiders" are of the Nineveh-kind, people we consider to be on the level of animals, brutal, destructive, is extremely hard to entertain. It is as hard for us now as it was for Jonah, as we shall see. Jonah may have entertained some small hope that when he cried his cry of overturning it would actually happen. Perhaps previously he had uttered the prophetic cry of judgment and the judgment had not come to pass. Psychologically, it cannot be an easy burden to bear to predict doom which never happens, even though from an ethical point of view one should be glad.

It is a thankless job to preach the word and never see it come out the way one tells it. Perhaps that is why Jonah hesitated in the first place. Jonah's word of judgment, the turn of the Ninevites, and God's act of repentance remind us of the essence of the Word. The essence of the Word of God is always the good news, even when it seems hidden under the bad news of judgment. God is who Jonah will later say God is, the God who is turned toward the world in everlasting love.

Harvest of Mercy
(Jonah 4)

It does not go over well with Jonah. In his disgruntlement, he eloquently describes his earlier motivation for refusing; he now wants to die. God simply asks him a question, "Are you right to be angry?" Whatever that may imply, to Jonah it meant apparently that his hopes are raised, for he locates himself in a place where he will be able to see what

will befall the city. Here, on the spot with a good view, the
final episodes take place. Jonah has some shade to protect
him from the sun but God lends a helping hand and as in
chapter 2 intervenes by "appointing," this time a plant
which will keep Jonah cool. Jonah's spirits rise but God is
not yet done and appoints a second creature, a worm this
time, which gnaws at the plant until it dies. The final appointing of God is that of a hot breeze to parch Jonah and
throw him once more into a fit of despair.

Then follows the final conversation between God and
Jonah, a conversation intended to make clear to Jonah that
God is in the right and has acted in character. We do not
know whether Jonah acknowledged this point and the book
ends with an unanswered question.

Guideposts

The story could have been over at the end of chapter
three, but it has a sequel, or second plot. Jonah is not left out
of God's concern. The prophet too has some turning to do. As
is appropriate to a parable the story ends with a question.
The question has the effect of addressing not only Jonah but
also all listeners throughout the ages.

The chapter is easily divided into two main episodes, vss.
1–5 and 6–11. The inside ordering of the structure follows a
neat pattern of speech and action arranged around feelings
(anger/gladness/anger). The speech takes the form of two
prayers on the part of Jonah, both of them requests to die
(vss. 3, 8). Three questions are asked on the part of God, two
concerning Jonah's anger (vss. 4, 9) and one concerning
God's own pity (vs. 11). The first action comes in response to
God's first question to Jonah (vs. 5) and God follows with two
divine interventions: giving the plant (vs. 6) and killing the
plant.

There are a number of things which take place three times
in these episodes. Jonah's feelings are mentioned three times,
he speaks three times, God speaks three times and acts three
times. There is as much movement in chapter four as there
was in chapter one.

Vss. 1–5 open and close with a mention of Jonah. For the
first time we hear something about Jonah's feelings. The
word *great* sounds here once more, as well as *evil*. Literally

the Hebrew reads, "It was evil to Jonah, a great evil." The line echoes vs. 2 of chapter one where we hear of the *evil* of Nineveh, that *great* city. As in chapter two Jonah prays, beginning this time with the same words as the heathen sailors' prayer, "Please Lord . . ." (see 1:14), one of the traditional ways of beginning a lament. The conversation in vss. 2–4 is set in the framework of vss. 1 and 5. For the first time we hear God and Jonah speaking in request and response. Before he petitions God, Jonah explains his motivation for his earlier refusal, which goes something like this: "Didn't I say so, that's why I fled, I knew it all along." What Jonah knew is revealed in the following line where he quotes one of those refrains of praise about God which are so rich and occur so regularly that they amount to credal praise: "A God, gracious and merciful, slow to anger and abounding in steadfast love, and repentest of evil" (vs. 2). In at least ten other places this praise occurs in the biblical material. A particularly interesting context of the line is found in Ps 145, where the balancing line reads "Good is the Lord to *all*" (Ps 145:8–9). Jonah knew indeed!

Only then does Jonah come to the petition which is uttered in the form of a request to die. The request is that of Elijah after his success at Mount Carmel and his persecution by Jezebel (1 Kings 19:4). God responds with a short question: "Do you do well to be angry?"

The next verse focuses again on Jonah, this time on his activity, by a series of verbs: "He went . . . , he sat . . . , he made . . . , he sat, . . . to see" (vs. 5). These actions are the response to God's questions which he does not answer. We note, last, that Jonah builds a booth which in Hebrew is a *sukkah*, reminding one of the booths of Israel in the wilderness.

Vss. 6–11 open and close with God. God "appoints" three times, the same verb that is used in regard to the fish that swallowed Jonah. Now God appoints a plant, then a worm, and then a sultry wind. *Appoint* is a technical term in this book for God's direct intervention in natural affairs. God causes a plant with an unfamiliar name to grow, a *qiqayon* plant, sometimes translated with "gourd." This God does, so the text reports, in order to give Jonah "shade for his head" and to "save him from his evil" (RSV "discomfort"). *Shade* is a symbolic word for protection in the Bible, also for the protection that comes from God. The word *evil* is used in all its nuances in this story as we saw already. Jonah responds to the plant with joy: "Jonah was glad over the *qiqayon* with great gladness." We note the parallel phrasing with vs. 1 of this chapter where Jonah is said to experience the salvation of Nineveh as a "great evil."

God next "appoints" a "worm," both a parallel and a contrast to the "great fish" of an earlier chapter. This worm gnaws away at the plant so it withers. Then, for the last time, God "appoints" something, a wind, as was done in the first chapter when God hurled the storm on the sea. Wind is expressed with *ruah* in Hebrew, the same word that is used for God's Spirit. As before the worm *smote* the plant, so now the sun *smites* Jonah's poor head (the verbs are the same in Hebrew).

Jonah repeats his earlier death wish. God then repeats the question asked before, with a small addition, "Do you do well to be angry over *the plant*?" (vs. 9). Jonah's reply uses some of the same words and exactly the same number of words as the question contains; "I do well to be angry unto death." (In Hebrew the phrase contains five words each time.) The final sentence of the book contains a small speech on God's part which repeats twice the verb "to have pity." Until now the word for aroused feelings has been *angry*; now it shifts to *pity*. Jonah supposedly pitied a plant in which he had no investment ("for which you did not labor, nor did you make it grow"), an ephemeral, inanimate phenomenon ("which came into being in a night, and perished in a night"). Then should God not pity Nineveh (note the repetition of "that great city"), full of human beings ("more than a hundred and twenty thousand persons") as well as beasts ("and also much cattle")?

The book ends with a question, which is suitable for a parable since the listeners are now faced with this question. In content the question recalls for us the question which ends the parable of the workers in the vineyard (Matt 20:15): "Is your eye evil because I am good?"

The good news has turned out to be the bad news, for Jonah at least. It is a great evil to him that Nineveh should be saved. He is so angry that he wishes to die and expresses this wish which is most unusual in the Hebrew Bible. We hear for the first time about his motivations and they sound genuine. He had known that God is good, in fact that God is good to all and that therefore Nineveh might be spared. The parallel with Elijah is interesting because Elijah faced the double-edged sword of a success which implied a failure. Jonah's success, the Ninevites' conversion to God, is at the same time Jonah's failure, his prediction is given the lie. God is successful, acting in character, "gracious, merciful, slow to anger," etc. . . . but God is in Jonah's eyes a failure. The word for anger with its harsh sound in Hebrew reverberates through this passage.

It seems that Jonah infers from God's question that the predicted destruction might happen after all. We may perhaps picture him, east of the city, with hope in his eyes. The words used for the makeshift shelter and shade are full of symbolic meaning. Jonah builds a *sukkah*. This shelter, with "all it represents in terms of the covenant with Israel and of remembrance of the unconditional election of Israel" (Lacocque, p. 87), is not enough. It needs an additional protection "appointed" by God and finally does not suffice at all when the God-appointed protection disappears and the sun smites Jonah's head.

The unlimited, free presence of God, represented by the *ruah*, has overcome Jonah. He utters his death wish again and again receives the question. This time he replies to the question, and God has put Jonah in position for the final point which is uttered in the form of another question.

The tone is throughout ironic. Expectations are created that are not met. Jonah had expected the salvation of Nineveh ("is not this what I said . . .") and yet not expected it. God, by the first question, creates the expectation that the announced destruction might happen after all. Jonah's hopes are raised again.

Next, he expects that the unexpected protection from the *qiqayon* will last but it does not. Appearances are created under which the reality of things hides. The sun's heat is, of course, not enough to make anyone want to commit suicide in earnest, and it is not really the heat of the sun which makes Jonah utter his death wish, but rather the heat of his anger. In Hebrew the verb for "to be angry" also means "to

burn." Jonah is not sorry for the plant at all, but he is sorry
for himself and his people, he pities himself. God has him
neatly cornered by this phrasing and set up for the final rhe-
torical question. The entire episode with the angry prophet frying in the
hot sun, as he was once tossed in the furious waves of the
turbulent sea, has a satirical aspect.

Suggestions

It is all too easy to condemn Jonah, to laugh at him, as
we have said before. What a petty bigot to resent the salvation of so much that is alive and a part of God's care! We
also said that parables are intended to call us, the listener,
to make a judgment. We should become alert when it seems
that we are judging the main characters in a story for their
failure. The identification should be with Jonah and we
should feel ourselves judged with him. We are not asked to
make a judgment on him, we are asked to make a judgment
on God.

Let us review the case. Nineveh, that great city, was a
nest of corruption and wickedness and posed a threat to the
people of Israel (see Hos 9:3; 11:5, 11, for example). Jonah
speaks the word of God in the city and the city is spared.
What we should keep in mind is that this sparing of necessity
involves a continuation of the threat to Israel; "through
Jonah's mission the enemy of Israel is paradoxically spared,
and is, so to speak, kept in reserve for further evil-doing
against Jerusalem" (Lacocque, p. 81).

Jonah might have been able to abide the thought of "the
nations" being under God's care and protection; he probably
did accept that idea. It became more difficult when the outsiders were a vile group, corrupt in the sight of all decent
people, a Hitler Waffen SS. Their redemption is all the more
unacceptable because their preservation poses a continued
threat to God's own people. On the surface we may laugh,
underneath we should perhaps cry. The problem of God's
justice is here presented in its complexity and its unac-
ceptability. The *ruah* of God has blown our sense of justice
out of the water. Jonah's anger is as natural and as human as
the anger of the workers in the vineyard, who cried "unfair,
unfair."

Some of the words in this part of the story remind us of a psalm in which it is said that God is Israel's protector: "Behold the One who keeps Israel,/shall neither slumber nor sleep./The Lord is your keeper;/the Lord is your shade/on your right hand./The sun shall not smite you by day,/nor the moon by night" (Ps. 121)."The Lord will keep, the Lord will keep...." Sure, sure.... that is what Jonah must have thought and felt, that is why his anger burns.

What about our day? What about our Ninevehs? The Lacocques make the point that for the audience of Jonah the question of Nineveh's destruction was not settled (p. 80). Are we still waiting for the destruction, are we still hoping for it, sitting with Jonah east of the city, counting on God's protection, the "shade on our right hand?" The preacher might want to address the question first at the point of those who are outside the Christian faith. Is it acceptable to us that God pours out grace over the unbeliever, over the Buddhist, the Moslem? Is it acceptable that God's grace goes out especially to those who are unacceptable to us straight, fair Christians? If we think that we can easily accept that point, then why are not more of those unacceptable groups visible among us?

Next, we can sharpen the focus by using the analogy of a particular group with an odious name among us—the Khmer Rouge, the SS, the white government of South Africa, the Kremlin, the Pentagon, depending on the congregation. If we cannot even accept "outsiders" into God's grace who have done us no harm, then how can we accept the grace of God going to those who are harmful to our well-being? To us then comes the question as it did to Jonah: "What about *you*? You are sorry for a plant.... What about *me*? Should I not be sorry for Nineveh, that great city, with in it...." Jonah did not labor over the plant or over the world. God labored over the world, which has not passed in a night and a day, and God pours out pity over all of it. The parable turns the accusing finger we had out to Jonah on ourselves. We mouth acceptance at best and do not live it. And God? The God who does not condemn Jonah but teaches him with laughter and tears running through the teaching, God turns that finger away from Jonah and away from us to point it at the heart of God's own self. The pity shown to Nineveh became the cross that shines in the world's darkness as the blazing sun which smote Jonah's head. All the world is God's and it is up to God to do with it as God wishes (Matt 20:15). Accept it into the wideness of God's mercy.

Bibliography

General
Alter, Robert, *The Art of Biblical Narrative* (New York: Basic Books, Inc., 1981).

Caird, G. B., *The Language and Imagery of the Bible* (Philadelphia: Westminster Press, 1980).

Crossan, John D., *The Dark Interval* (Allen, Texas: Argus Communications, 1975).

Frye, Northrup, *The Great Code* (New York: Harcourt Brace Jovanovich, 1982).

Good, Edwin M., *Irony in the Old Testament* (Philadelphia: Westminster Press, 1965).

Gottwald, Norman K. (ed.), *The Bible and Liberation* (Maryknoll, NY: Orbis Books, 1983).

Ruth
Campbell, Edward F., *Ruth* (Anchor Bible; New York: Doubleday, 1975).

Trible, Phyllis, *God and the Rhetoric of Sexuality* (Philadelphia: Fortress Press, 1978).

Esther
Moore, Carey A., *Esther* (Anchor Bible; New York: Doubleday, 1971).

Moore, Carey A. (ed.), *Studies in the Book of Esther* (New York: KTAV, 1982).

Jonah
Fretheim, Terrence E., *The Message of Jonah* (Minneapolis: Augsburg Publishing House, 1977).

Lacocque, André, and Pierre-Emmanuel Lacocque, *The Jonah Complex* (Atlanta: John Knox, 1981).